C000174097

Build It!.....With Pallets

By Joe Jacobs

The Good Life Press LTD

Published by The Good Life Press Ltd., 2009
Reprinted 2010

Copyright © Joe Jacobs

All rights reserved. No parts of this publication, including text or
illustrations, may be reproduced or stored in a retrieval system, or
transmitted, in any form or by any means, electronic, mechanical,
photocopying, recording or otherwise without prior permission of the
publisher, The Good Life Press Ltd.

The plans within this book are the intellectual property of the author and
are offered for use on a not for profit basis.

ISBN 978 1 90487 143 9
A catalogue record for this book is available from
the British Library.

Published by
The Good Life Press Ltd.
The Old Pigsties, Clifton Fields
Lytham Road
Preston PR4 0XB

www.goodlifepress.co.uk
www.homefarmer.co.uk

Set by The Good Life Press Ltd.
Illustrations and photographs © by Joe Jacobs
Printed and bound in Great Britain
CPI Antony Rowe, Chippenham, Wiltshire

Acknowledgements

I'm indebted to all the people who I blagged pallets from. Special mentions go to Ash and the crew at Howarth Timber in Malton who provided some that were actually made of useful wood as opposed to matchwood. After conception of the book I must thank Charlie for introducing me to his next door neighbour Ron Hugill. Ron has kindly shared some of his own pallet project work with us and relieved me, for one, of the burden of having to make one of absolutely everything listed herein.

Preface

If you enjoyed Build It! then you'll find entertainment from this volume. Equally vice versa. Somewhere in between the first book and its second edition in progress, the publishers decided in the course of our random Build It! discussions that a book devoted solely to the recycling of wooden pallets was a worthy cause. Here it is. For those lovers of more technical gimmicks averse to quasi-carpentry, don't worry; Build It 2! will be out soon.

I freely confess that I am a great lover of finding uses for items for which they were not originally intended. Take for instance an old wooden cross-pein hammer with the head resting on the floor and the steel cross end wedged under the bedroom door. A better doorstop one could not want. The handle points upwards to the ceiling as it restrains the open door and it even looks rustic.

Whilst some objects can be reused or recycled without modification, most recycling will invariably require some degree of material alteration. In the process of finding uses for wooden pallets about my smallholding, and subsequently writing about it, I have come to the conclusion that these items represent a vast material resource waiting to be exploited. Pallets are dumped, broken up and given away and quite often they have only been used once in their short

Build It!....

miserable commercial life. Well are they any good? I hear you ask. Well, some are, some aren't. Those that don't make the grade also happen to make great free firewood for the log burner.

DIY is supposed to be fun, especially if you aren't quite sure what you'll end up with. Don't despair if things don't work out right the first time as pallet wood is free. Pick up the bits and start again or dismantle another pallet.

These DIY books are not intended as rigid sets of blueprints but as vaguely inspirational guides for some daft ideas of your own. Whilst my hands are not those that do dishes, and are covered in scratches, callouses and blackened nails, if you work in the health-care or beauty sector you might want to invest in a pair of chain mail gloves. Ailing projects lead to the shops.

Lastly, neither the author nor the publishers take any responsibility for accidents or disasters resulting from attempts to replicate the projects illustrated in this book or perceived or real shortcomings of the plans. The plans and intellectual copyright of these ideas are offered only on a not for profit basis.

Joe Jacobs
Yorkshire 2009

Contents

Other ideas – Further discussion and helpful pointers for you to try out the following projects:

Garden Trays, Bird Nest Box, Go-Kart, Toys, Sheds, Picture Frame, Hanging Shelves, Bike Rack, Rabbit Hutch, Hay Rack, Lamb Creep Feeder, Boot Remover, Steps and Ladders, Sea Chest/Blanket Box, Dog Kennel.

Build It!....

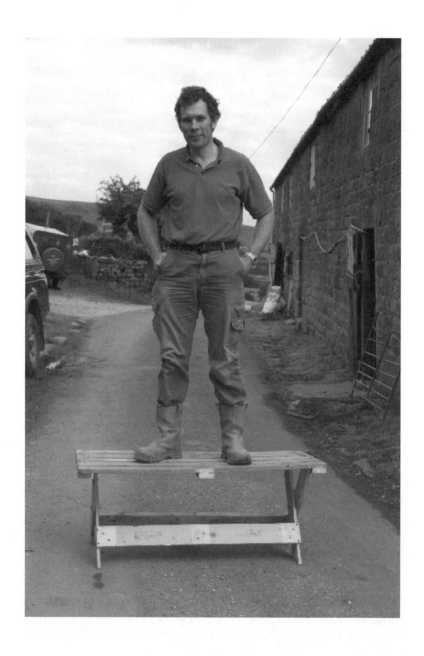

Introduction

There are three methods of obtaining wooden pallets:
1)   Use of a pickup truck in broad daylight
2)   Use of a pickup truck after dark
3)   Politely asking for them

All three methods could be said to work, although politely asking for them is my personal preference.

These days wooden pallets are everywhere. The burgeoning road haulage industry needs them to speed up the loading and delivery of just about everything. You can get a pallet of goods sent almost anywhere in the UK for fifty pounds. There must be a lot of pallets out there working very hard, so hard in fact many of them are now only built as use once and throw away. What a waste. In a world where natural resources are dwindling at an alarming rate, I suspect it's only a matter of time before the price of timber starts to climb dramatically. Wood shouldn't be thrown away unless it's genuinely rotten or has been cut up to the extent that it is no longer usable. Along with mass pallet production so their overall quality seems to have dropped, but the humble pallet need not have such a short life as the timber in many of them is fit for a wide variety of uses. Pallets are most definitely available for nothing, you only have to ask politely. Don't be put off by broken ones, there's still plenty of good wood in them. What should be said however is that the thinner the pallet wood, the more likely you are to break it whilst trying to dismantle the pallet. Some pallets are obviously made of quite good quality timber with a nice grain to it, others are simply knocked up out of any old knotty bit of wood close to the maker's hand. Dissecting a pallet can be done in several ways but does require some tooling and a modicum of patience. The timber that isn't fit for much makes excellent free fuel for a wood burner or multi-fuel stove. Sound interesting? Then read on. Take a trip through any industrial park and you'll see pallets everywhere. In many cases companies are paying skip and recycling businesses

Build It!....

a lot of money to get rid of them. Some of the stronger types are reused but typically once a plank gets broken, they are binned. Most companies will let you take broken pallets, many will even give you complete ones. Builder's merchants will always have a broken one or two that you can have.

Types of Pallet

There used to be some sort of standard in pallet size and construction, but that's long gone. Put half a dozen pallets next to each other and you may find there are no two alike. The basic anatomy of a pallet is as follows: firstly, pallets are made to be picked up by forklift trucks and are therefore designed to keep the load above the floor so that the forks can get in underneath. Some pallets are reversible and have planks on both sides. The reversible type are usually strongest and have a series of three or four spacing bars made from 3 or 4" timber which form the gap between the two sides. It can be difficult to get these planks away from the spacer bars. The second type of pallet (there could be more) has its plank top resting on a series of wooden blocks (usually nine); these blocks sit in turn on a bit more plank framework.

I will interject early on that taking a pallet to pieces is not half as simple as it looks. They are held together by annular ringed nails or staples that are designed to grip the timber thus holding it together. With this in mind, it should be evident that a spindly matchwood pallet may not survive the deconstruction process. If you have an option, go for the pallets that have the strongest, thickest planks with the least knots in the grain. Indeed, there are occasional rogue pallets floating around made from half decent imported hardwood; great timber but a devil to take to bits. With a little practice you should be able to get at least half the planks off the pallet without snapping them. We'll discuss deconstruction techniques a little further on.

Tools

Most of the projects in this book can be completed with a basic set of tools although power tools don't half make the job a lot easier. These days tools are cheap. Have a look around B&Q's budget range or find a discount tool shop and you will see what I mean. Some of the cheapest tools really aren't bad at all as Chinese quality control appears to have come on leaps and bounds in recent times. A selection of hand tools is essential. Here's a short guide for the uninitiated on the bare necessities required for simple woodworking projects.

Whilst the quality of some cheap power tool brands is debatable, these machines can cut huge swathes of time out of DIY projects. You can carry out these projects without power tools but it takes a lot longer and will require far more in the way of blood, sweat and tears.

Hand Tools

A basic toolkit should comprise of at least the following:

Crowbar – You'll need at least one of these to get the pallets to pieces. I bought a set of five bars for ten quid. One for almost every occasion.

Build It!....

Hammer – There are various designs but a claw hammer is about the most use for this type of woodwork. The claw enables you to remove all those bent and mis-hit nails from your project.

Screwdrivers – Cheap screwdrivers don't last very long as the heads are not usually hard enough. A selection of flat and cross head with hardened tips is useful. Alternatively, cordless drill/drivers are handy but they do require frequent recharging.

Wood Saws – A couple of useful wood saws (not old blunt ones) are essential for project work. A tenon saw is the short type with a reinforcing strip along its top edge, very useful for short straight cuts where accuracy is required. A general purpose cross-cut saw (the bendy, two-to three-foot-long type of saw) can be used for anything from cutting plywood to sawing through heavy timbers.

Hacksaw – Necessary for cutting anything made of metal; there is a tensioning wing nut on the saw which tightens the blade. The saw will not cut correctly unless the blade is properly adjusted. A Junior hacksaw is also a useful addition to a toolkit and can be used to cut in situ metalwork where there may not be enough room to wield a full size saw. Very useful for sawing through obstinate nails that are holding your pallet together.

Spanners – A selection of spanners typically covering 6, 8, 10 and 12mm are useful for projects where bolts are a better design option than screws. A couple of adjustable spanners may suffice equally well.

Pliers – There are many designs of pliers, and they may be used for anything from loosening rounded nuts and bolts to pulling nails. A standard set will be of help in pallet projects.

Punches – A steel punch can be used to either lose nail heads into the workpiece, or punch out existing broken nails through the workpiece.

Portable Workbench – Useful if you don't have a fixed one. The type with the handles and adjustable tops can also be used for clamping glued pieces of work. A long workbench with a vice at each end can be a great boon for holding objects for cutting or drilling.

Vice and Clamps – If you are using glue in your projects a vice and or clamps may be handy. You can usually buy clamps in discount tool shops for a couple of quid.

Measurement – A steel rule, a tape measure and a set square for marking 90 and 45 degree cuts should be in your toolkit.
Sandpaper – Can be used to smooth off rough wooden edges. If things look really bad and power tools are not available then a Surform is probably what you need. Sandpaper comes in a myriad of grades. It's probably best to buy a pack of mixed grade sheets then you'll hopefully have all eventualities covered.

Knife – In addition to the obligatory pocket knife a sharper type of craft knife is useful. Most jobs require the use of a knife even if it's only to open the awkward packaging of a box of screws. The thin snap off blade variety never seem to last very long. The Stanley knife design is a better option and is more controllable in the hand.

There are plenty of other tools that are desirable for DIY projects, but the only one that I personally would not be without is my Yankee screwdriver. Manufactured by Stanley tools the Yankee is a long ratcheted changeable-bit screwdriver. When you push down on the handle, the tool bit rotates. Yankee screwdrivers require some physical effort to operate, however they are far quicker to use than putting in screws using a conventional driver, and unlike cordless battery models they do not require frequent recharging.

Power Tools

There are some very good power tools on the market, but there are also some very bad ones. Hopefully this short guide will help you to make a selection that doesn't end up wasting money. There are some very big names in power tools with corresponding big prices, although arguably you get what you pay for. Many of the cheap Chinese import power tools come with spare drive belts and motor brushes which is daft because the product will have ground itself into the dust long before the spare parts are needed.

Big companies like B&Q and Homebase cannot afford to have their names ruined by poor products and therefore spend a great deal of time sourcing decent budget power tools. All the electric power tools I have purchased from B&Q's basic range have served me faultlessly for several years. Many of the other cheap imports I have used have died very quickly indeed. In some cases (especially large angle grinders for some reason) tools have packed up within just a few hours of being put to work. If an item appears to be particularly cheap and plastic looking then buy something else.

Drills – These days you can buy an electric drill to suit almost any occasion, although in reality one is probably all you'll ever need. I've fallen out of love with cordless battery products because I always forget to put them on charge. Buy a variable speed mains drill and it shouldn't see you far wrong.

Electric Saws – There are a plethora of designs of electric saws and all are useful, but some more so than others. A jigsaw (or pendulum saw) with a selection of blades can be used for most project woodcutting applications although they do not have the greatest cutting speed in the world. Circular saws are not ideal for accurate cutting work although they come into their own for rip sawing and cutting straight lines in large sheets of plywood. They are great for breaking up pallets. It is now possible to buy a small portable bench saw for as little as thirty pounds. To my mind these are a better investment than a circular saw. Essentially the two are the same anyway except the saw is upturned and mounted into a metal bench. Instead of having a circular saw mounted in a bench, it is possible to have one mounted over an adjustable table. These are known as mitre saws and are available as fixed or sliding. Sliding cross-cut saws are extremely useful for cutting timber to a precise angle, e.g. 30 degrees, 45 degrees etc. The limitation of a cross-cut saw is that it is only possible to cut timber up to about 1' (300mm) wide with a sliding saw and perhaps as little as 3" (80mm) wide with a fixed mitre saw. To somebody with no power tools whatsoever I would suggest that a jigsaw is a very useful piece of kit and that a bench saw would also make a good investment, although a circular saw would make a cheap alternative to the bench variety.

There are inevitably rough edges that ought to be removed from wooden items and sandpaper, files and planes are all great for this, but if it's a large job then electric planes and sanders really come into their own. Sheet sanders are cheap and are an effective way of achieving a smooth finish on wood that is not overly rough in nature. If the timber is particularly rough sawn then a plane may be more suitable for smoothing work. For jobs where the removal of a significant amount of material is required then a belt sander could be what is required, but these devices need particular vigilance when in use as they will literally eat through your creation in no time at all.

Lastly, it is possible to feed pallet wood into a bench planer or thicknesser and have it come out looking like new. A planer thicknesser is a large electric self-feeding bench plane; feed a tatty looking piece of pallet into one side and watch it spit a nice piece of wood out of the other side. At this point it's worth interjecting that nails and metal fragments left in the work piece do nothing for the condition of powered planes and sanders. Be sure your timber is free of metal before taking a power tool to it. We'll discuss this machine and its application later on. It is a great tool for cleaning up old wood but is probably not a worthwhile investment for most pallet DIY.

Fixings

I've generally used a combination of 1¼" (30mm) and 2" (50mm) oval nails, and 1½" (40mm) screws to fix things together in this book. However, to all you novice woodworkers there is something of note. Many of you will be familiar with PVA glue which is great

Build It!....

for both woodwork and making Christmas cards. What you may not be familiar with is PU glue. Polyurethane glue sets in about five minutes and is extremely strong and so is very useful for rapid moving woodwork projects. It cures on contact with moisture and expands slightly in gaps (like the cans of expanding builder's foam). It can easily be trimmed and sanded too. Buy it in mastic gun tubes and remember to put a cap on it when you've finished using it. The other thing of note is that when trying to produce an item that's supposed to be half decent looking, a tube of wood filler may not go amiss. Plug holes and gaps with the stuff and then sand it down later.

Working Safely

Having rambled on about a few of the tools necessary to construct DIY pallet projects, it might now be worth dwelling on a few of the pitfalls awaiting the unwary.

Eye protection is paramount for most practical jobs. The discomfort of sawdust in the eye is nothing compared with what could happen if the random wood fragments thrown out of a power saw hit home. We only have one pair of eyes so protect them. The protection of hearing is widely forgotten. Whilst you may not consider a noise to be particularly loud, prolonged exposure may be damaging your hearing. Earplugs are cheap. If working in a confined area, wood dust can also become a major irritant to the respiratory system. Unfortunately, it really is the power tools which are to blame for fine sawdust and there are times when a simple cheap face mask may be a real advantage. Airborne sawdust is also a major fire hazard. Whilst woodwork is difficult if wearing gloves, there are projects listed herein that will require them. Rigger gloves and nitrile dipped builder's gloves cost about ninety-nine pence a pair and don't half save your hands from wear and tear.

Perhaps the biggest risk when working with power tools and extension leads is that of electrocution. Very few people know the state of the earthing system in their house and whether it really represents a more attractive pathway to electricity than the hapless tool holder. If your electricity system is not fitted with an RCD (residual current device) then you would be well advised to get one as it will offer a degree of protection in the event of chopping through your wires. An RCD will cut the supply in the event of it detecting current leakage to earth. RCDs are now available as in-line units and may even be incorporated in some extension reels. Fire too could be a potential hazard when working indoors; there is little to say apart from be aware of the potential hazard of overloading electrical circuits with lots of devices plugged in simultaneously. Small low cost fire extinguishers are available for about ten pounds and, along with a first aid kit, represent a worthy workplace investment.

I undertake many woodwork projects al fresco when the weather's nice. If you have a heated workshop, great! I don't. Provided that it's not raining or overly windy, I much prefer to strew my tools around a large open area and construct projects in the fresh air.

Units of Measurement

Everybody seems to know what a length of 4 x 2 is. If I were to offer you a piece of 101.6 x 50.8 you wouldn't have a flaming clue what I was on about. Many things in life come in imperial measurements; the way I see it, both units of measurement have their place and can quite happily co-exist. If you are unsure there are 2.54cm to an inch.

Both standards of measurement are referred to in this book. I refuse to quote something as 81.3cm when 3' would have sufficed, or 15.75" when a simple 40cm would have done. Where possible I quote measurements in both units.

Build It!....

Taking a Pallet to Pieces

There are several methods of dismantling a pallet, but not all methods seem to work for any individual unit. It is necessary to own a decent hammer and a pair of fine prybars, crowbars or wrecking bars. A circular saw is very handy but for the less dangerously minded, a good sharp cross-cut saw is also good. If embarking on a project that requires the wood to be planed, sanded and generally tidied up, you must strive to avoid leaving metal nail heads in the planks: pull or punch them out. Metal fragments in the wood quickly ruin planes and sanders and are hazardous to one's general well-being if airborne at high speed. The reason that a pallet doesn't fall to pieces when carrying a load is that the nails used in its construction are designed to keep it tight. For the layman the whole nail is covered in ribs (a bit like a screw but it doesn't screw) and this provides a great deal of resistance to withdrawing the nail and doesn't aid easy dismantling. Quite often pieces of hardwood will be used as spacing bars in between the layers of planking and fairly fresh pallets will definitely come to pieces with less effort than older ones.

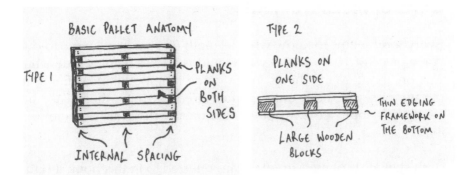

As you can utilise sections of pallet in your projects in their entirety, it's worth trying to match particular pallets with particular projects. When taking pallets to pieces, first have a good look at the way the nails are driven in and the way the planks are arranged. You can then adjust your design and plan accordingly. Sometimes the planks at the ends are more difficult to remove so I tend to start

16

with all the middle ones first. The blocks or spacers that separate the top side of the pallet from the bottom tend to prise away from the planks fairly easily. I've got loads of the large square blocks in a pile but I've yet to find a use for them other than fuel. Maybe if I save enough they'll make building blocks for my kids or they might machine into a giant Jenga set. As pallet wood is often of a poor finish we also have the option of attempting to tidy it up a little or using it in its raw form.

After much persevering I've come to the conclusion that it's often expedient to sacrifice two inches off the ends of a pallet by sawing through each plank as illustrated. This saves time as it only leaves the central spacer(s) to be prised off from the planking. Stubborn blocks or spacers may be split with a hammer and chisel to reveal the nail inside, thus allowing it to be pulled out of the plank. Sometimes you will find that you've pulled the head from a protruding nail. The only remedy for this is the use of a vice on the remaining nail stub. Nails can be saved and reused in some circumstances. I tend to prefer using oval nails as they are less prone to splitting what can sometimes be delicate pallet wood.

Inevitably de-constructing pallets creates a great deal of scrap and offcuts so if you don't already own one, go and get a wood burning stove (or wait for Build It 2! and make one!).

Treatment

At the end of the day, a pallet is a pallet and you are not going to somehow turn it into burnished walnut. Pallet planks vary in quality but what is certain is that collectively they will have enough nail holes in them to furnish a small cheese. What you do with these holes is up to you. Some may prefer to fill them using a purpose wood filler or alternatively sawdust and PVA, while others may prefer the authentic recycled look. Do remember that if your creation is intended for the outdoors, holes represent points at which water will ingress and rot your hard work. Give the timber a good coating of wood treatment if you want it to last. As you will be aware, many old pallets have some type of stain, paint or dye on them; I can recall having seen a lot of blue ones for some reason. The dyes can be difficult to get rid of, even with persistent planing and sanding. In one project several parts of the product ended up with yellow-coloured planks, and so I thought it best to paint the rest of the job yellow. No honestly, it's only going in the garden and it doesn't really look that bad. Whatever colour you elect to paint your finished product, give it a thorough coating to ensure some degree of longevity.

Adaptability

This paragraph is of paramount importance to the whole book:

Some of these projects require a degree of adaptability on the part of the interpreter. I might be using a piece of pallet wood that is 4" (10cm) wide and ¾" (19mm) thick. You might not have a piece of timber that matches that description. Working with pallets you have to match what you have got with a general idea; precision engineering or brain surgery this is not.

PROJECTS

And so to the crux of the matter, which is to actually make something of use out of an old pallet. I say 'of use' in the most light hearted of tones as this is intended to be a simple getting started project, but even simple projects have a habit of not always turning out as one might have first envisaged them. Don't worry, the pallets are free and even the nails are reusable.

1. Hurdles

If you are not aware of what a hurdle is outside of the 110m Olympic event, it is simply a short section of fencing or gate. The beauty of hurdles is that they are lightweight, movable and can be tied to each other and used to make temporary fences, pens and crushes to hold sheep, pigs or other animals. They also work for kids. When it comes to working with animals you simply cannot ever have enough gates and hurdles. Used in conjunction with plenty of 'band' (baling twine for those not in the know) and a sharp pocket knife, gates and hurdles are used for fencing, gathering, sorting and treating livestock. The willow screening variety you see in garden centres is perhaps the oldest incarnation and is still used for sheep

Build It!....

in some parts of the country. Hurdles come in practically any size but typically they will be 4, 5 or 6' long and high enough to prevent a sheep jumping over them. Regardless of whether you keep sheep or not, these items can come in handy around the garden, allotment or smallholding.

In their basic heavy form pallets can be used for making small enclosures. The type of pallet that is closely boarded on both sides is very useful for making temporary chicken runs for growing birds. Three or four pallets and a bit of netting on the top and the birds generally cannot escape. Pallets of a more lightweight type (ie. not so closely boarded) can easily be turned into lightweight hurdles. Use a claw hammer or a crowbar to carefully prise off the boards from one side of the pallet. Turn the pallet over and reattach them, filling in the gaps between the other planks. Longer pallets allow for a longer hurdle and a more useful finished article.

To construct a traditional type of wooden hurdle you need eleven lengths of pallet wood. Many basic pallet planks are 4" (10cm) wide. If you have an appropriate saw you could just use six planks split down their length. Whatever you decide, four pieces should be 3' (90cm approx.) in length, which will be used for uprights at either end. Five lengths should be 4' (122cm), or as long as you can get. The remaining two pieces are for diagonal cross bracing. You will need plenty of nails but the construction of the hurdle itself is fairly self explanatory. Just look at the diagram.

SIMPLE HURDLE

2. Raised Beds

With all this 'five fruit and veg a day' business and what's been termed an economic downturn, there's never been a better time to start growing your own vegetables. The Victorians did a great deal of gardening in raised beds. Apparently they were able to cultivate higher growing temperatures year round, hence increasing productivity. Raised beds are a great way of making small neat enclosed areas in which plants or veg can be grown. I've also used these beds to help tidy up unsightly garden areas and make use of otherwise unusable slopes and banks in the form of terracing.

To make a raised bed a wooden retaining wall can be built on a permanent or temporary basis. The construction technique that I favour is to bash wooden posts into the ground and then use the wooden planks on the inward side of the bed. A raised bed wants to be at least 18" (45cm approx.) deep. Backfill the created space and ensure that it contains sufficient depth of usable soil. Some plants will require more root depth than others.

The sturdy central spacer stakes that the pallet boards are nailed to make suitable posts for the corners. Start by knocking in a row of these posts in a straight line. Position the posts every 1m and use a plumb line or a piece of rope to ensure they're in the correct place. If you are making a square raised bed, the weight of the soil is contained by the walls providing they're suitably nailed at all the corners. If you are building a raised bed against a wall or bank, posts will need to be driven in well in order to contain the soil pressure on the walls of the bed. Use pallet planks that are as thick as possible. I have chanced upon some fine 1" (25mm) thick ones. If you want a raised bed to last a bit longer you could try lining the woodwork with some sort of plastic membrane to stop the damp getting to the woodwork. Timber treatment does cost a little extra but does also drastically increase product life.

If you have any old window frames you can easily turn a raised bed into a cold frame. I have previously added some old window

Build It!....

frames to the top of a raised bed which we then grew strawberries underneath. This stopped the chickens getting to them. If you don't have any window frames, make a framework out of pallet wood and cover it in some sort of transparent or horticultural polythene. The only problem with enclosed raised beds and cold frames is that you must remember to water the plants that are in them on a regular basis.

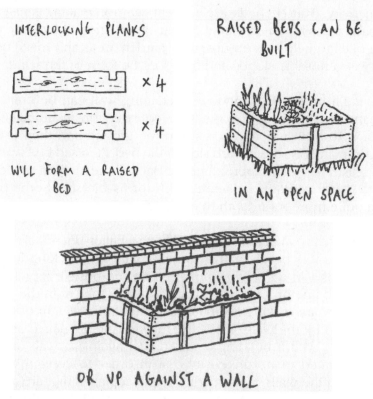

RAISED BEDS – square, lean to, notched ends.

If you can be bothered to prat around notching the ends of about eight equal length pallet planks as illustrated you can produce a set of boards that will interlock (a bit like a traditional log cabin). This is a very cheap method of making a movable raised bed set (or a run for a guinea pig or rabbit) that comes apart and requires no fixings.

3. Fencing

Photo courtesy of RH

Pallet wood does readily lend itself to making up sections of fence. Let's face it, it's about the same dimensions as the fence planks you can buy at cost from the timber merchants. Where it does fall down is that it is untreated and has more craters and holes than the moon in which water and rot can get in. If you are going to use pallet planks for fencing, treat it lavishly. I'd already used pallets for fencing prior to this experimental novel, as will many of you. When I saw Ron's fence, however, I was particularly impressed. Firstly, he'd managed to make it out of fairly substantial pieces of pallet timber that would last, and secondly he'd added some regularly spaced pieces of 'pretty' saw work which gave the fence a bit of a visual edge over the efforts I've tried and tested.

A basic length of fence can be made on two parallel bars. Obviously, the longer the bars, the longer the section of fence. The upright staves should all be accurately cut so that they are the same length. 3' (0.9m approx.) is fine. What makes or breaks a nice fence of this type is the care taken to cut all the points the same. Mark all the saw cuts on each plank and then you will end up with a set of regular looking angles. It doesn't matter what pitch you cut the top of each plank to, as long as it's as regular as the next plank. When you've cut all of your points, all of the planks should be nailed to the two horizontal bars at an equidistant spacing. I'd use a spacing that was the same width as the planks I was using, although there's no set rule. If you are making a longer fence then you will need a method of joining your sections of prepared fence together. My advice is

Build It!....

Photo courtesy of RH

to use a wooden post and cut the top off to a point so that it matches the rest of the fencing. In the accompanying photo you will see that a piece of 1½" (40 mm) box-section steel has been driven into the ground in lieu of wooden posts. In order to connect posts to the fencing you do need a drill that will drill bolt holes in steel. The most effective part of the project is the saw-cut wooden tops that have been inserted into each of the metal posts. If you have an electric jigsaw you could replicate this or invent your own design for such an idea.

4. Gate

If you are making a section of fence you might need a gate. Indeed, a very quick garden gate can be fashioned out of most types of pallet simply by using the correct saw cuts. In the illustration given the type of pallet used was the variety that has planks over four bracing bars. I cut both ends off the pallet as discussed in deconstruction and then removed all the planks and nails from one side. I used a power saw to thin down the 4" thick pallet spacers left on the rear of my workpiece. I reduced them to about half their thickness. What I was left with

was a gate-sized set of planks attached to two rear thinned down bracings. From the picture it should be clear enough. The real strength in any gate lies in the diagonal cross bracing which can be added afterwards. Remember that the lowest end of a diagonal bar on a gate is the hinge side. These diagonals are what stops gates from sagging over time. They help transfer the load of the gate back to the hinges and gate post. It's worth ensuring that when making a gate you spend a little time to ensure that the saw cuts on the diagonal bracing are accurate. You want joints that butt together nicely against the other timbers. If you want to make a nice picket sort of gate as described in the fencing section, carefully mark and cut all the planks to a point along the top edge of the gate.

5. Sheep Trough

After something of a simple start we'll now look at something a little more complex. I needed another sheep trough because at the time of writing I have a load of heavily pregnant ewes which are being fed concentrate food rations. It might interest you to know that as the unborn lambs grow they press on the sheep's stomach and reduce the space available for food. Concentrate sheep pellets help the sheep to get more grub out of less bulk. For those of you without ewes, fear not; a sheep trough also makes an equally good garden ornament.

I decided to make a long sheep trough that would allow plenty of hungry mouths to congregate around it. For the gardeners I'd suggest that you might only want to make a single trough as long as your average pallet plank which is about 4' (1.2m) in length. It helps if you can find a pallet with wide planks. 6" (15cm) wide is ideal and they do exist. You will need three planks in reasonable condition for the floor and two sides. You will also need another piece from which you can make the ends. The feet for the trough can be made from offcuts, although the central pallet bracing bars are usually made of a harder material and are fit for such a purpose as 'feet' which will probably be perpetually damp.

Build It!....

Start by cutting three of your widest planks so that they are all the same length For the purposes of a measurement we'll say the trough will be 1m long. 'Imperialists' can make a yard-long trough if they wish. If you want a trough with square sides it's a simple enough task to nail or screw the sides to the floor of the trough to form a gutter shape. If you want a traditional-style trough with flared sides you will need to saw or shave both edges of the trough's bottom board. If unsure consult the diagram.

SINGLE SHEEP TROUGH

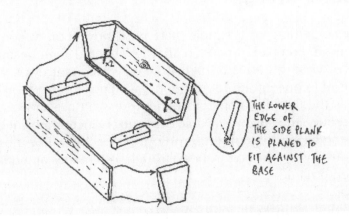

THE LOWER EDGE OF THE SIDE PLANK IS PLANED TO FIT AGAINST THE BASE

To make the ends of the trough, having screwed the sides and floor together, measure the gap at either end of the trough and cut corresponding pieces to fit. Feet should be substantial enough to keep the trough clear of the wet ground. One wooden block at either end

will do for a short trough. Use screws through the floor of the trough and into the feet underneath.

As I made a double-length trough, I simply doubled up on the material requirements. The two halves were joined together with a 12" (30cm) or so block positioned lengthways underneath the trough and acting as both a joiner and a middle foot. I also cut another piece of timber the same dimensions as one of the ends and screwed it in place in the middle of the trough. The structural strength of my long trough is maintained by having a length of timber underneath the trough and a central internal block that both halves are fixed to. You'll see it in the pictures.

27

Build It!....

6. Planters

Planters may well be the easiest of pallet creations that you can make. You can use them for growing flowers or vegetables in, or you can use them simply as storage bins. What is certain is that the collective cost of purchasing planters from commercial outlets makes them an attractive project for the would-be grower with a spare couple of hours on his or her hands. You can make planter projects either as complicated or as easy as you like. When you are working with pallet wood don't prematurely throw away your offcuts as it's these shorter pieces that often lend themselves best to making many of these garden pieces.

Planter One

Photo courtesy of RH

Again I must reiterate that the idea of working with pallets is to adapt the design idea to the pallet you have to hand. This cuts down on a lot of excess cutting of planks to fit specific design dimensions. This first design was made from planks that were 4" (10cm) in width, but other sizes will suffice. Start by making a base for the unit. Cut three 1 yard (90cm) long planks and lay them side by side. Cut two short lengths of plank to act as feet which will fit under your three base planks – about 12" (30cm) long in this instance. Position the feet so that they are about 6" (15cm) inwards of the base ends and nail your three base planks to them. Refer to the sketches as appropriate. To make the planter illustrated in the photo, mark and cut your baseboard as per the diagram. At this point I'll say you could leave it square and continue with the same idea.

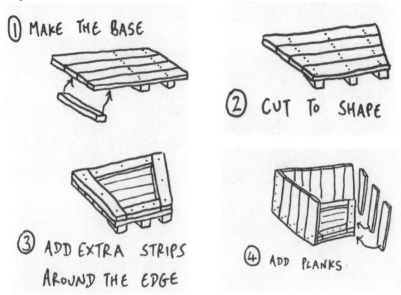

The edge of the baseboard requires some reinforcing to give a body of wood that the sides can be nailed onto. The width and thickness of this edging is not particularly important. You can use more pallet planks if you want or other offcuts. Try and get the joints between the adjoining pieces of edging fairly tight, ie. cut them at the correct angles. The depth of the planter is again open to interpretation, but in this instance we'll say 12" (30cm) planks should be used. If you've stuck with the general measurements outlined in the design you will need about twenty-two of these short planks. Use two nails per plank to fix the planks to the baseboard, making sure they are sitting squarely and upright before nailing them. If you don't take the time to get the first few planks on nicely, the planter will end up looking like a dog's ear. You may have to trim down one or two finishing planks to fit the inevitable final gaps. Use nails at the corners to join adjacent planks together.

Build It!....

The project is finished with a continuous edging around the top, which acts to hold all the planks in place. You will need to find, or saw to size, some pieces that are about ¾–1" (20–25mm) wide and ½–¾" (15–20mm) thick. You'll need about 7½' (2.3m) of edging in total. Again, to make a nice job you will need to ensure that you get the corners measured and cut so that they are flush along the top and butt up nicely against each other.

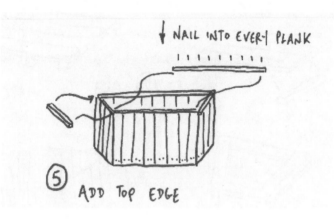

↓ NAIL INTO EVERY PLANK

⑤ ADD TOP EDGE

Planter Two

This rather ornate device can be made with or without the artistic flair of the pictured design. It's simply a long box on legs. It's probably easiest to start making either a square or trapezoid shaped box as illustrated in the previous example. To make a set of legs for the aforementioned project get four lengths of the timber used in between the planks. This stuff usually measures about 1½ x 3" (35 x 75mm) in cross section and is fairly substantial. Cut the four legs to a length of 2' (60cm). Cut one end of each leg as per the diagram. These cuts will ensure that the weight of the trough and its contents has support from underneath. The

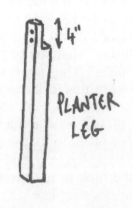

4"

PLANTER LEG

legs should be attached to the trough with coach bolts or substantial wood screws. Pre-drill the holes for these before joining the legs to the body.

Photo courtesy of RH

The rather nice example in the photo has been made using short sections of the 2" thick timbers used in between the pallet.

Planter Three

If you don't mind spending a bit of time sawing, you might like to try making containers out of blocks as demonstrated by my new found pallet enthusiast friend Ron. The methods of construction illustrated in the two photos are easy enough to replicate.

Photos courtesy of RH

Build It!....

This is a very easy way of making up nice containers. I should, however, point out that in both cases the components used in each layer need to be of regular thickness. In both cases all angled cuts are 45 degrees. Most cross-cut saws have their plastic handles moulded so that you can use the handle as a 45 or 90 degree measurement gauge. Neither of the pictured examples of the block-built planters were very large, perhaps 1' (30cm) across. Both would have bottoms made by nailing on pre-cut boards to the underside. You will have to experiment a little to satisfy your own needs, but you should be able to get the general idea of building in layers and nailing to the layer beneath from the photos provided.

There are other quick and easy ideas you can experiment with in order to grow plants. The quickest idea I came across by accident would make a nice herb window box for what amounts to little more than three saw cuts and half a dozen nails. Saw off one slice of pallet along the inward edge of a plank. See the corresponding photo. Remove a plank from the remaining pallet and nail it to the bottom of the box. It really can't get much simpler.

7. Compost Heap

In times past I have seen other people use pallets and similar scrap wood to successfully make composting enclosures. I have also tried it myself. Whilst I appreciate that they do not work as well as modern plastic products, they are both free and are relatively environmentally friendly. My brother-in-law had a whole row of such pallet-made enclosures, although I think he's now sacrificed them for plastic ones on the altar of progress.

Compost heaps work well with plenty of grass cuttings and suchlike. Muck heaps don't generally function in the same way. You need plenty of plant matter to speed the composting process up. Use three similar pallets to make a rear and two sides. Take a fourth pallet and chop it down a third to make a slightly lower front. You can rob boards from one side of a pallet and fasten them to the other if your pallet is not particularly closely boarded. You can make a more permanent enclosed heap by driving four stakes into the ground with intermediates if necessary and nail your boards to these stakes.

PALLET COMPOST HEAP

8. Bird Table

Having just moved house, there's an old post with a small platform nailed to it outside the kitchen window. This is the remnants of what was once a bird table. I thought it might be nice to knock up a new feeding house out of a few leftover scraps from one of the other projects. It certainly wasn't difficult or time consuming to make and will hopefully keep both the birds and the kids happy.

Build It!....

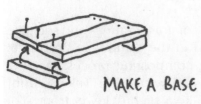

As always, start by making the base. I used two pieces of 4" (10cm) width plank cut off to 14" (35cm approx.) in length. Split an 8" (20cm) long piece of plank lengthways to make two pieces about 2 x 8" (5 x 20cm). **MAKE A BASE** Mount the two 14" (35cm) base pieces on top of the two smaller pieces, one at either end. Use nails as appropriate

The ends of the bird house were made from more of the same planking. Four lengths of wood were cut to 12" (30cm). Two pieces of wood are used to form each end. An apex for the roof should be marked onto the planks – see the diagrams if you are unsure. I made a 90 degree apex for simplicities' sake. The ends of the bird house can be nailed onto the ends of the baseboard using two or three nails per plank.

ADD SIDES

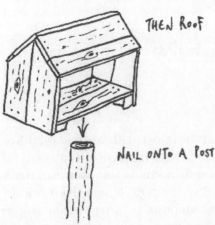

THEN Roof

NAIL ONTO A POST

To make the roof you will need another two lengths of 4" standard plank cut to 16" (40cm). You will also need a couple of 16" (40cm) lengths that have been thinned down a lot, one to about 2" (5cm) in width and one to about 1¼" (3cm) in width. It's perhaps easiest to nail on the top of the roof first. Use the two larger pieces of timber before having a quick measure and ensuring that your two thinner roofing timbers are the correct size.

With the addition of a few screw-in metal hooks around the base to hang nut containers, you have a bird house. With the addition of a small hole in the top of each gable end, a rope could be added and the table could be hung from a tree. Alternatively, a fencepost or suitably long stake can be driven into the ground and the table nailed to the top of it. Just make sure it's high enough to dissuade the local cat.

9. Outdoor Table

In the following example I used parts from two separate pallets. One pallet would probably suffice if you were a little gentler with it than I was during the deconstruction process. It does help if you have found a half decent pallet to start with. What I have engineered here is a piece of outdoor garden furniture; I designed it as a small picnic table to go with some chairs in the garden. As the finished item ended up as quite a strong design, it could also be utilised as a garden bench. In the process of building this project I used an electric drill, a circular saw, two bolts and twenty screws. So, in terms of resources, this idea certainly doesn't require a vast amount.

Build It!....

Whilst I spent several hours pontificating various design and building strategies, I would suggest that by following this design idea you could have a finished table in two to three hours (but please don't hold me to that).

From a selection of pallets I looked for one that had planks that were regularly spaced and in nice condition. I selected a section of pallet that had a regular gap of about 1½" (4cm) between each of the planks. From the photo you can see that this section was cut out from the rest of the pallet to provide us with a ready-made table top. The downward side of the table top still had some large blocks of packing wood attached. These were not needed and were simply prised off.

Legs for each end were made out of pieces taken from another pallet. By cutting four lengths of wood to approximately 26" (66cm) in length, the pieces for the legs were formed. I marked the centre point of each of the pieces and drilled a ¼" (6mm approx.) hole through each leg. Using a ¼" (6mm) bolt, or whatever else you have that may be suitable, join the leg planks by bolting through the pre-drilled holes. The pieces should now form an adjustable X shape.

I designed my table to sit at about 18" (46cm) high. The length of the legs was calculated so that the table sat at the design height. Using legs of an X arrangement there is a little leeway in adjusting

the height of the table up or down prior to fixing. Each set of legs will need trimming top and bottom so that the legs will sit flush with the underside of the table and with the ground. Each set of legs will need cutting according to the width of your table; rest one of the Xs against one end of the table top and mark the angles that you will need to cut. Hopefully, if you do want to try making one of these, a quick reference to the photos will make things a little clearer. All the legs should be identical when you have finished. Note, however, that if you don't drill the hole dead in the centre of the plank that things could go a little awry later on.

Each set of legs is fixed inwards of the ends (see photo) of the table and are screwed to the pieces of timber that run across the width of the project. I used two substantial 1¾" (45mm) wood screws to secure each leg. At this point you will realise that in the process of forming a crossed set of legs, one leg will be offset out of line of the other and will require a packing piece. The packing piece needs to be of the same thickness material used for the legs and serves to fill the gap between the out of line leg and the point of fixing. Fix the packing piece in place with a couple of screws before situating the legs in place.

The legs were braced longitudinally with two long planks which were secured to them using wood screws. I considered fixing cross bracing to both of the X legs but opted instead to use a single cross bracing timber joining the two lower planks together at their mid-point (again the picture paints a thousand words).

10. Garden Chair

Once you get into the subtle nuances of working with pallets, you will notice that you can cut them up into many different types of section that can then be incorporated into a design. I had considered building a planed up posh sort of chair but then, whilst analysing a pallet that had four solid spacing bars inside it, I realised that if I cut it in a certain way the sections of pallet would quickly make a rustic outdoor chair.

It's fine writing a description but in this particular instance, unless you get the saw cuts in the correct place, the thing is by and large a complete waste of time. Reference to the pictures and diagrams will help you replicate this project. First find a pallet with plenty of 3-4" (7.5-10cm approx.) type boards on it and four internal separating timbers. With the pallet standing on one end the pallet planks will be horizontal, or parallel to the ground. The spacing blocks that are inside the pallet will now be vertical, pointing up and down. Cut out all of the planks from the centre section of the pallet (on both sides) to effectively leave two mini pallets. In my case these two mini pallets ended up 39¼" (1.0m) in length and 17¾" (45cm) wide. By turning the pallet into these smaller usable sections we can now make a simple chair.

One of the pallet sections will be the back of the chair. In this particular example the back was 39¼" (1.0m) high. The other similar section is cut in two to make both the seat and the front legs. The sitting height of the chair should correspond to a comfortable height for its principle user. 17-18" (45cm approx.) in height will be about right for most people's needs. In order to achieve this height take into account that the seat top is about 4" (10cm) thick and the legs underneath will therefore need to be shorter than 17¾" (45cm). I cut my section into two pieces, both measuring 15" (38cm). One of these sections will make the front 'legs' and the other section the seat.

CHAIR SECTIONS
FIT TOGETHER
LIKE
So

The whole affair is joined together using nails and wooden offcuts applied to the chair sides. The seat top goes on top of the legs. I cut eight pieces of 15" (35cm) long plank to secure the sides of the chair and another two of 19¾" (50cm). Two pieces of plank secure the front legs to the seat and two pieces connect the seat to the chair back. It's not worth describing other than in diagram form – see the illustrations. The remaining pieces fill in the jigsaw with the

Build It!....

NAILING THE
SHADED WOOD
TO EACH SIDE
HOLDS THE
CHAIR
TOGETHER

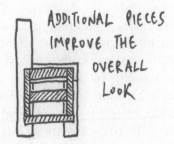

ADDITIONAL PIECES
IMPROVE THE
OVERALL
LOOK

19¾" (50cm) plank joining the front legs to what are best described as the rear legs. I am well aware that some readers are infuriated by a lack of numerical preciseness but I make no apologies. The pallet wasn't made precisely in the first place, so neither are these ideas. In many instances I just nail on whatever is to hand and don't bother measuring until I attempt to write up the idea: this is extreme woodworking at its very roughest.

I used a pretty ropey old pallet to make my chair and so I guess it could do with a coat of paint before being left outside. With a slatted seat it might be a mild improvement to fill in the gaps with some cut down wood. This would be a little more comfortable on the derrière (that's French for backside!), although a cushion would probably do just as well with considerably less work required.

11. Bench

This particular project turned out to be my favourite one in the whole book. I'd got my hands on some pallets that were made of very nice quality pine with very few nails in them and with planks almost 1" (25mm) thick. Fortunately the pallets came to pieces fairly easily, and because the wood was not overly rough in nature I decided to manufacture a piece of furniture that wouldn't look out of place indoors. I settled on the idea of a bench as we often seem to run out of seating when people with kids come round.

The bench seat comprises of two pieces of pallet plank that, when butted and glued together, measure 35⅜ x 9" (90 x 23cm). Glued to the underside of the seat top is a framework that gives the bench strength and provides recesses in which the legs sit. The framework is made from the same ¾" (22mm) thick planking as the bench top, but cut into ¾" (3cm) wide strips. The following pieces are needed to make the framework: two 1¼ x 35⅜" (3 x 90cm) (1 3/16 x 35 3/8 in) and six 1¼ x 7⅜" (3 x 19.4cm) (1 3/16 x 7 5/8 in) pieces. The lengths are critical to the design but the cross sectional sizes are not, so go with what you have to hand.

Build It!....

I found that clamps were handy when gluing the framework to the bottom of the seat planks. Nails would do just as well (with added glue) as nobody's going to be looking at the underside. Obviously four pieces (two long, two short) are glued around the edge of the seat bottom. The remaining four short strips are used to make up two separate slots that the legs will glue into.

Mark the position where the bench legs will fit at 10" (26cm approx.) inward of the ends of the bench. Using this marked

position, leave a gap wide enough for a leg plank, ¾" (22mm) in this instance, to fit into and then glue the remaining pieces of wood to the seat bottom to leave a slot for each leg.

To make the bench legs I used more of the same pallet planking. As mentioned previously, this was a quality pallet (if there is indeed such a thing) and the planks were 5½" (14cm) wide. I cut two lengths of 17¾" (45cm) for the legs, two 9½ x 1½" (24 x 4cm) pieces to the make feet and a length of narrower 4" (10cm) plank to make a crossbar. The crossbar piece must be an exact measurement of the distance between the legs when they are in position. In this case the crossbar measured 15⅜" (39cm).

At this point I got carried away and decided to cut out some love hearts in the legs with my jigsaw. It seemed like a good idea at the time but I put them too high up the legs to be visible under normal circumstances, so it ended up as a bit of a wasted opportunity. I used a ¾" (20mm) flat-bladed wood drill to make two holes next to each other (centres at ¾" (20mm) apart). This leaves the top of a heart shape and then only the bottom of the shape needs marking and cutting with the saw. You could easily make a trefoil pattern in the same way.

The feet required a little saw work so that they looked a bit more foot like and not just like blocks nailed to the bottom of the legs. The feet are there to provide stability to the design. I removed two 1¼ x 2" (3 x 5cm) wedges from each of the foot blocks and sanded some of the visible top edges and corners; this made the two blocks a little more attractive. The feet were both glued and nailed to the legs. The feet sit on the outward sides of the legs and are mounted flush with the bottom of each leg. Both feet have two nails driven into them through the bench legs from the inward side.

The hardest part of joining all the pieces together is marrying up the pair of legs and crossbar so that when it is fastened it will fit into the slots underneath the bench seat. Obviously, both legs need to be marked to find the central position that the crossbar will be fixed to. The crossbar was positioned 3½" (9cm) up from floor level and on the centreline of both legs. I drove two nails through each leg, one above the other, the first 4½" (11cm) from the floor and the second at 6¾" (17cm). Nails are from the outward side in. Both nails are on the centreline of each leg and serve to catch the ends of the crossbar. Before the nails are fully hammered home into the crossbar, add a helping of PU glue, ensuring that the whole thing is sitting squarely well before the glue dries.

The last job is to nail and glue the undercarriage to the bench top. If you've got it all correct, the two should marry up quite nicely. Use PU glue in the slots and ensure that the legs are positioned centrally on both sides. Drive down two nails through the top of the bench into each leg, measuring carefully to ensure that your nails don't miss the top of the legs. I ought to add, as a note, that to produce a decent finish to the project you really need to use oval or lost-head type nails. I used a metal punch to drive all my nails into the wood and then put a small smear of pine coloured wood filler over the top.

The project was concluded with a fair amount of sanding work to tidy up the rough edges. I'm torn between wanting to treat the wood with a tin of antique wax and painting it a nice bright shade of bottle green. The only downside to the bench is that it is just about long enough and strong enough to hold two adults and is thus attractive to the potential sitter-down as a 'shift up mate' type of bench. However, I have witnessed from afar that if one person stands up suddenly, the other does need to reposition himself immediately if left sitting outward of a leg. With hindsight you could set your legs a little further out. I shan't be looking for a job in IKEA's design department just yet.

12. Shelving

I've just moved to a much larger smallholding/farm and have inherited a colossal workshop which I'm very pleased about. In all honesty the workshop is probably about eighty feet long and needs a fair bit of furniture to make it usable, not to mention storage facilities. I thought that I'd get off the mark by constructing a simple set of shelves that I can cover in junk or use to stack tools on. Once you get the gist of the shelving idea, you can alter the design to produce all manner of shelving; it wouldn't be too difficult to make a nice greenhouse staging unit.

I got started with this idea by looking for a way that I could cut up a pallet to leave me with a pair of ready-made shelving unit sides. I settled for cutting off entire slices of pallet that were two planks wide and still had the spacers left in them (refer to the photos). I took two of these slices of pallet and removed the planks from one side of each section. Ensuring that the protruding wooden spacer was free of nails, I thinned the spacer bar down a bit with a circular saw (see photos) until, instead of being 3 or 4" (7.5 or 10cm) thick, it was only 1½ to 2" (4 to 5cm) thick. These sides were now both ready with included shelf supports. The pallet I selected would make a shelf that stands 42 " (1.07m) high. Obviously this height

Build It!....

measurement will be completely dependent on the size of the pallet you had to start with.

Rob the rest of the discarded pallet for its planks which can be used to make the shelves; I needed three planks per shelf. The planks for the middle shelf were cut to 39½" (1.0m approx.) in length. The top shelf measured 41" (1.04m) to allow for a slight overlap of each end in the interests of neatness. The shelving planks are regularly spaced with a small gap between them (so they're no good for storing your marbles on). I've used two screws per plank end to secure them. The depth of the shelves ended up as 10¼" (26cm). When it comes to fixing your shelves in place you are best off starting at the bottom and working upward, thereby giving you the maximum screwdriver manoeuvring space at each level.

The final thing the shelves needed was a couple of diagonal braces on the rear. These act to lock the shelves in a fixed position and without them they will just sway around and lack any sideways rigidity. I used two pieces of thinned down plank (about ⅜" (15mm) thick and 1⅜" (35mm) wide), cut to a length of 26" (66cm). From the photos you will see that these battens are secured along the top shelf's rear edge and down to either side. Use one screw in each end to secure them, thus making the shelves stable.

I was pretty happy with the net result and the unit will do fine in my shed. I would suggest that if the shelves were to be used on a slightly uneven floor the sides might need the addition of a set of feet in order to further improve stability. If you increase the thickness of the unit (by perhaps having sides that are three or four planks deep), you could turn the idea into a simple workbench or plant staging.

13. Workbench

As we live on a farm there are occasional butchery jobs that get done. Usually it's just game and poultry, but there have been the odd larger jobs. I bought a butcher's block for the purpose of cutting stuff up, but it was in very nice condition, and sitting on a tidy wooden frame it has now become more of a piece of indoor furniture. We did recently cut up a pig, and in the planning process I fully intended to have this bench ready for the job. Sadly it wasn't. Next time I have a butchery job to do the workbench will be waiting, that is unless it's been hijacked for some other purpose.

The bench was concocted out of the type of pallet that has a closely boarded top, about nine small wooden blocks underneath and a little more plank framework below that. Because the pallet was made from nice solid inch-thick timber and was closely boarded, I decided to cut it up to make the table top and use some of the remaining pieces to fill in the gaps in the table top boarding. I cut the pallet so that instead of having nine wooden spacer blocks underneath, it only had six. This left the pallet measuring 47¼ x 18½" (1.2 x 0.47m). I took a fair amount of care in measuring and planing  the pieces required to fill up the gaps in the table top. I did achieve a very tight fit and also added a few nails for good measure. I used a nail punch to countersink the nails into the table top and used wood filler to fill the holes and gaps. When the filler had cured I gave the table top a good going over with an electric sander.

The legs were all made from my pile of discarded pallet spacers. By this I mean the wooden bars that separate the two sides of the pallet. If you do likewise, make sure you get all the nails out of the legs before sanding or planing them. The legs were sawn to approximately 1" square (40mm² approx.), but anything slightly bigger is fine if you've got the timber spare. Cut all the legs to 35½" (0.9m).

I made up a set of boards that would allow the legs to be bolted to the table with a high degree of structural strength. See the diagram. In this case the table was 18½" (47cm) wide. Two boards were cut corresponding to the width of the table. The boards were made from some of the same 5½" (14cm) wide planking as the table top. A little cutting and sanding was done to the ends of the table top to ensure that a board would sit flush against each end.

Two legs were attached to each end board using ¼ x 3" (M6 x 80mm) coach bolts. The legs are fitted on the outside of the board. Two coach bolts were used per leg and the bolts were passed so that the washer and nut are tightened against the leg. After drilling and alignment the bolts were removed and a slight countersink was made in the end boards to hide each coach bolt head. With the coach bolts in place but the legs not attached, the end boards were carefully nailed to each end of the table. The coach bolt heads will now, of course, be inaccessible, but the threaded bolts protrude from the ends of the table ready to accept the legs.

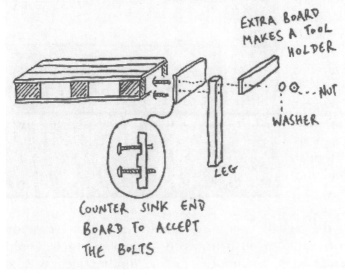

EXTRA BOARD MAKES A TOOL HOLDER

NUT

WASHER

LEG

COUNTER SINK END BOARD TO ACCEPT THE BOLTS

Build It!....

In order to get top strength between the end boards and the table top, I drilled two 5mm holes (using imperial, go slightly less than your ¼" bolt size) through each end board and into the wooden

spacer block behind. I then screwed a ¼ x 3" (M6 x 80mm) bolt into each of these holes. With these in place there is no danger of any of the end plate nails being pulled out. I've sat on the table and it would easily take twice my weight. It's an easy job to put the legs on and bolt them up. It was at this point that, as an afterthought, that I devised a small tool rack for each end.

In the absence of me having nothing less than ¼" (80mm) coach bolts, the project was left with four bolts sticking out at the corners. At first I did consider sawing the bolts down until..... Cut another length of plank to the same width as the table and drill two holes in the plank

corresponding to the protruding coach bolts. You can now push this piece of timber over the bolts and bolt it firmly against the legs. Look at the pictures if in doubt. Repeat for the other end if so desired.

I thought the bench was a resounding success. I did toy with the idea of putting a posh front on the pallet which would have almost rendered it an indoors table. Another idea was to turn the characteristic pallet front into drawers. I did also toy with the need for bracing boards on the legs. In time extra boards might be required but as we have a sturdy kitchen table that doesn't seem to need them, I didn't think I'd bother either.

14. Barrow

This was a very nice idea I got from Ron who makes these photogenic barrows using pallet wood and old chicken shed wheels. You might have difficulty getting hold of old steel wheels if you don't live in a rural area. They usually show up at farm and machinery auctions and can often be seen rusting gently in fields attached to very old chicken sheds and sheep feeders. You could, however, get away with a modern wheel of sufficient diameter. It's up to you whether you use this idea to create an ornamental barrow or whether you decide to construct one that might be of some use.

Making the main framework for the barrow isn't too onerous; it's actually built around little more than an H shape. The H frame is pulled in at the wheel end and is therefore wider at the opposite end, giving a set of ample handles with which to push it. The two long bars that run from the wheel to the handles measure 53" (1.35m). These bars need to be made of substantial timber, either a spacer bar from inside a pallet, or possibly a slimmed down one anywhere between 1½" square (40mm²) and 1½ x 3¼" (40 x 80mm). If you don't have any pieces that you consider long enough, join two lengths together with an overlap of about 12" (30cm). Use coach bolts to make the join and hide the overlap under the body of the barrow.

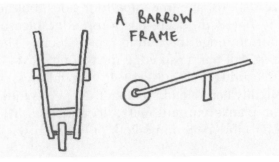

A BARROW FRAME

Build It!....

You'll need an axle of some description for your wheel. Assuming you haven't got a metal wheel, you can buy a plastic or pneumatic one for between five to ten quid (you could even make a wooden one – see footnote immediately below). Buy a ¾" (20mm) bolt or use a piece of broom handle for an axle.

To make a wooden wheel, refer to the bucket base instructions. Make two of these bases and glue them together.

At the front of the barrow, the overall width of frame extremities is 9½" (24cm) and at the handles end the overall measurement was 15¾" (40cm). Measure and add a 10½" (27cm) and a 12" (30cm) bar into the barrow frame to keep the two main beams apart. A set of legs should be cut 13" (33cm) in length, using similar timber, and screwed or bolted to the outside of the frame; position them 1 yard (90–95cm) from the wheel end of the bars. At this point in the proceedings you should have a basic frame and legs which you can drill to take an axle and a wheel.

The next task is to make some sort of a body. It's entirely up to you whether you wish to make the project look decorative with some wavy edges or fancy woodwork. You could just plank out some of the frame like the old railway porter's barrows. In the example given the load box measures 29" (75cm) in length and has slightly flared sides. Make up the box and then fit it to the base is the best method. The sides on the barrow illustrated are 7" (18cm) deep, but you could adjust this to suit.

Cut enough 29½" (75cm) lengths of plank to form the two sides. The ends are trapezoidal in shape (meaning four sides, but not square). The front end is 7" (18cm) deep, has a top edge measuring 15⅜" (39cm) and a bottom edge measuring 10¼" (26cm). The rear end is 7" (18cm) deep, but has a top edge measuring 17" (43cm) and a bottom edge measuring 11⅜" (30cm). If you nail this lot together you will get a slightly flared load box that then needs turning upside down and some planks cut and nailed to the base. The box can now be screwed to the main framework of the barrow.

In Ron's example he added some little infill blocks mounted on the framework against the box. These are only small wedges of timber, but make for a nice overall impression. The handles should be shaped to some degree with a saw and some sandpaper, but this really depends on whether the item is purely decorative or for practical use.

Photo courtesy of RH

15. Trellis

The types of trellis sections you can buy in the shops are usually made of fairly insubstantial timber and the ones that are well made tend to cost a lot of money. The simple answer is to make your own sections of trellis. Admittedly you do need a power saw to cut each pallet plank into three or four lengths, but they probably cost less than a shop bought trellis. To make a simple square or rectangular growing trellis you will require plenty of strips of pallet wood, some screws and a screwdriver. The spacing of the bars and the eventual finished size is entirely up to the designer. I have pondered and experimented with trellis design before, but hadn't done anything great due to a lack of need. Whilst debating pallet architecture with our friend Ron (give the credit where it's due), I took some photo's

Build It!....

Photo courtesy of RH

of two of his designs which we've included here.

The first idea is for a trellis that can be fastened to a wall or fence with the plants growing out of a container set at the foot of it. It's dead simple and only requires eleven strips of wood. Cut your planks into strips that are between 1¼ and 1½" (30 and 40mm) wide. You'll need four 4' (1.2m approx.) strips for the uprights and the following shorter lengths for the cross members: 2⅜, 23⅜, 25½, 27½, 31½ and 33½" (60, 65, 70, 75, 80 and 85cm). 'Imperialists' among you might want to regularise the measurements a little. Use either oval nails or suitable screws.

Make up the four sides using the following pieces: 4' (1.2m) for both of the sides, 21⅜" (55cm) at the bottom and 33½" (85cm) at the top. Add the two remaining 4' (1.2m) lengths so they are arranged at a regular interval. The shorter horizontal bars should be added as appropriate at positions every 8" (20cm) along the trellis sides.

Trellis idea number two is for an interesting unit that was designed to take a garden tub. The unit has a simple base that allows a sack trolley to be placed underneath. In this way the user is able to move his or her plants and trellises around their patio or garden. To make this you will need plenty of thinned down pallet wood as for trellis design number one. The base is made using five 20" (50cm) lengths of timber nailed to two pieces of spacing block cut to 16" (40cm) in length. Space the five bars at regular intervals or alternatively just have a solid plank floor. The trellis at the rear is rectangular and is made from four 4' (1.2m) uprights and eight 20" (50cm) cross members. The trellis is nailed to the back of the base. To give the trellis some support, a diagonal bracing bar is nailed to each side

Photos courtesy of RH

of the structure. These bracing bars measure 34" (86cm approx.) in length and are attached from the front sides of the baseboard to a point about half way up the trellis. See the photo for the general idea. Use screws for a secure joint.

16. Hanging Larder for Curing and Food Preservation

Having finally just got around to experimenting with home-cured meat, many of the recipes I have used ultimately end up with the instructions "and find a cool place to hang your *** for several months" (insert bacon, ham or sausages as appropriate). This is all very good, but as most homes have some form of central heating these days it isn't very practical advice. I have found several breezy cool places in sheds and outbuildings but even so, I'm not convinced of the security of my porcine delicacies over the lengthy periods of time that I'm waiting for them to mature. I thought it a grand scheme to invent a simple hanging larder to keep the birds and

Build It!....

insects off my future dinners. Whilst admittedly not everyone might try making bacon, the project does indeed add a little diversity to the book and might also come in handy if your fridge ever breaks down.

Obviously you are going to need some fine net and 16' (5m approx.) of strong cord (or thin rope) as well as pallet wood for this project. An old pair of net curtains or voile would do nicely for the netting. Start by finding some of the thinnest ¼–½" (10–15mm) pallet planks you have got and make a floor that measures 16 x 16" (40 x 40cm). You can make it bigger if you want. Use two supports under the floor. If you are using 4" (10cm) planks (use 3" (7.5cm) if you've got them), you'll need six 16" (40cm) lengths to make the stated size floor. The separate framework at the top of the larder can be used for hanging curing meat and keeps the net away from the food. The top frame should be made from similar timber to the floor and the overall dimensions should remain the same as that of the floor. You'll need four lengths of 16" (40cm) plank and three 16" (40cm) lengths of plank cut or thinned down to 1¼" (30mm approx.). The thinned down bars will be used to make hanging rails. Make up another square out of the four lengths of plank and fasten them with glue, screws or nails. Bear in mind that through each overlapping corner you will need to drill a small centrally located hole; position your fixings accordingly. The three thinner bars for hanging items should be evenly spaced and fastened in place as shown in the diagram.

You will have to drill four holes in order to rope the two frames together, one above the other. Put one frame on top of the other frame and drill a hole in each corner area, taking care to avoid the nails. By drilling down through both the upper frame and the floor at once you should have all the holes aligned. Take a 100" (2.5m approx.) length of rope, form a bight (a U shape for all ye landlubbers) and thread both ends of the bight through a pair of neighbouring holes in the underside of the base. In short, shove two separate Us of cord up through the base. You will need to put a stopper knot in each of your four lengths of rope before you thread the top frame onto the rig. With the top frame threaded on, tie all the four loose ends together and hang the project up before adjusting your stopper knots and levelling it all up.

Use a continuous bead of glue around the topside of the upper frame and size and glue in a piece of fine net or mesh. The remaining framework is covered with net that should hang down like a tube over the framework. The net is not fixed underneath the wooden floor, but is long enough so that it can be tied shut with a length of cord. Use glue and staples to attach the mesh to the edge of the top frame. If you need to create a joint between two smaller pieces of net the answer is a strip of duct tape on one or both sides of the seam.

I've hung bacon and suchlike wrapped in muslin, but if the juices seep through the flies will still land on it and may even lay if you're unlucky.

With this re-invention of the wheel, items can be hung from the top bars using S-hooks or placed on the lower tray. As long as your net seams are good, the flies should be kept away. Mmmm...... Prosciutto. I can hardly wait!

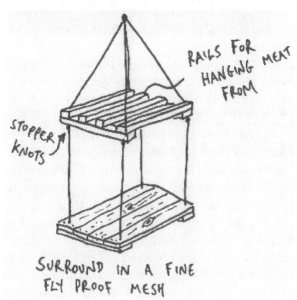

RAILS FOR HANGING MEAT FROM

STOPPER KNOTS

SURROUND IN A FINE FLY PROOF MESH

Build It!....

17. Poultry House

If you've never kept chickens, then in these days of growing interest in food, where it's come from and its general sustainability, there's never been a better time to start. I have a load of nice looking rare breed hens but quite frankly as regular egg layers they are an utter waste of time. Every seventy-two weeks most commercial egg producers get rid of their flocks for new ones. It's not that the chicken has anything wrong with it at seventy-two weeks other than a graph showing that it starts to eat more food. Four hens in a shed, nay one hundred hens, make little difference to a feed bill at seventy-two weeks and a day or even three years. The small man's concern is not quotas or graphs but simply that he has happy hens that lay eggs. Ten thousand hens in a shed do eat a lot more after about seventy-two weeks and so economics dictates they have to go. If you want chickens that lay eggs, go and find a chicken farm, be it a battery unit or otherwise, and buy half a dozen balding, henpecked birds when they change flocks. The birds will soon feather up, lay lots of large eggs for several years and they will only cost between fifty pence and a pound each. I've just bought another twenty birds for seventy-five pence each. Now that's chickens going cheap. I've even included the details of the Battery Hen Welfare Trust in the Resources Section at the back to help get you started!

You couldn't write a book for this intended market without having a chicken or a duck house in it anyway. The trouble is this. I've written so many articles on building chicken sheds that I now have more poultry houses than chickens. With another two books lined up in the near future my chicken houses are now breeding like rabbits. And now for your delight and entertainment, I've just made another one... Here it is.

This bird house would easily hold three or four birds, but it doesn't have a nesting box. The snag with chickens is that most of us keep our small flocks for eggs and if you don't want dirty eggs then you are going to have to keep the house clean and put a small nest of hay or straw in a back corner for the birds to lay on. This design is for a house with a single pitch roof that slopes from the front down to the back.

When you're building a house of any sort it's always best to start at the base and work upwards and wooden chicken houses are no exception to this rule. I started by making a slatted floor as I've found over the years that they aid cleanliness and don't get quite so mite infested in the summer. I cut an area of slats out of a pallet that measured 24¾ x 22" (63 x 56cm). The base consisted of about five planks mounted on two 24¾" (63cm) lengths of spacing wood about 1½ x 3" (35 x 75mm) deep. I worked out that I would need about seven planks for each of three sides with a different arrangement on the front. The planks nearest the front of the shed measure 24½" (62cm) and the rearward planks measure 20" (51cm). All the rear side planks were 20" (51cm).

Build It!....

In most of these designs, the overall finished dimensions are governed by the availability of sometimes just one critical piece of wood. Working with new wood one would not normally set out to design items of 20" or 51cm in length. It is frustrating at times trying to convey this to the reader who may expect cast-iron guidelines, so please don't hold it against me. The pallets have spoken!

① MAKE A BASE

② NAIL ON SOME PLANKS

③ CUT THE SIDES AND REINFORE ALL OF THE TOP EDGES

④ FILL IN THE FRONT

⑤ A DOOR

AND A ROOF

⑥

I nailed all of my side planks onto the base before I marked and cut the pitch of the roof. Use two screws or two oval nails per plank. The rear planks did not need cutting as these were already the correct length. You will find that you have to trim a closing plank to fit the final gap on each side. I marked the pitch of the roof along each side with a straight edge and then cut it. The height at the front is 24½" (62cm) reducing to 20" (51cm) at the back. Nail the corner planks to each other down their edges. Because all the side planks are only fastened to the house base and not to each other, they need a reinforcing bar along the top edge. I nailed a piece of narrowed down pallet wood onto the inside top edge of each side. Nail from the inside outwards and make sure all the planks are fastened to this bar. Providing you have nailed the

corner planks together as well, the three sides of the house should be rigid.

The front of the chicken house can be made the same way as the rest of the structure as long as you leave a gap for the door. I altered my pattern slightly to accom-

Build It!....

modate the wood I had left, thereby nailing on horizontal boards instead of vertical ones. From the photo you will see short boards either side of the door and these are fastened to an internal piece of batten. In order to form a doorway and give the planks above (and next to) the door some support, fix a length of batten to the inside of the front panel at a height that corresponds with the top of your doorway. I made my doorway to be 6¾" (17cm) wide by 8½" (22cm) high. The length of batten used on the inside of the panel was positioned so that it protruded down about ½" (10mm approx.) into the doorway; this stops the door from opening inwards. This arrangement can be seen in the photos.

A door was made from a couple of short offcuts of plank with a strip nailed across the hinge end to hold the two halves together. This is

illustrated in the photos. I used short screws to attach a hinge to the door. Top tip: When using screws close to the edge of a piece of woodwork, drill a pilot hole first or else you will split the timber. A wooden door catch can be made from another piece of scrap wood. I used a 5" (12.5cm) long stick of 1" square (25mm²) to make a turn-buckle mounted on a single screw. At this point in the proceedings I was running out of decent pallets and so the roof was made from whatever lengths matched the need, regardless of either width or thickness.

The roof measures 2' x 27⅜" (61 x 69cm) and has two other lengths of pallet wood 19½" (50cm approx.) long holding it together on the inward side. All the individual roof planks are nailed to the internal crosspieces. The crosspieces are set on the underside of the roof so that they are just inward of the front and rear edges of the roof. You will have to measure this so that the pieces just slot inside of the house walls when the roof is put on. My roof was made of quite heavy timber so I haven't added any additional means of securing it.

Chickens don't like getting wet and this roof is not of a design that is completely watertight. I'm going to add a square of roofing felt to the top of my chicken house, but a square of plastic and the use of a staple gun would suffice equally well. Despite the sides being vertically planked, they will keep the weather out to a sufficient degree, but if you're not happy with yours you could caulk the seams with filler. There are just two further ideas left that you might wish to incorporate: the first is to add a small partition or tray in the rear of the house to act as a nesting area. The second idea is to cut a length of timber for a perch 2' (61cm) long using 1" square (20–25mm²). This can easily be fitted by driving a nail through each side of the house so that it catches the ends of your perch bar. Finally, treat your house with paint or a wood preserver if you want it to last. Give some feathered friends a home today.

18. Poultry Crate

I've lost count of the times that I've been at poultry sales and seen people with birds in cardboard boxes where the bottom has got wet and gone soggy; it's happened to me as well. Cardboard boxes work fine where you only have two or three birds to transport, but try cramming many more into a box and you risk the bottom falling out. Get ten chickens in a big box and you've got a fair weight on your hands. To avoid the potential pitfalls of chicken transportation, make yourself a simple poultry crate and avoid the hassles of trying to find a suitable box for the job every time you need one. This idea was always included in my intended scope for this book, and no sooner had I actually made it than I heard of the aforementioned budget chickens and the crate got its first outing. I only put about half a dozen birds in the first time it was pressed into use as the rest of the posse went in a bigger crate; that said, it would easily take ten birds for local short duration trips.

As usual I started by making up a floor, on this occasion measuring

39⅜ x 15¾" (1.0 x 0.4m). I used four lengths of plank and nailed three 15¾" (0.4m) plank pieces crossways underneath, one under each end and one length under the middle of the floor. Use some of the same material to make some uprights. Cut six 12½" (32cm) lengths and fix these in place as uprights, two at each end and two in the middle. The uprights should be attached with two screws or oval nails and are positioned so that they butt against the extra pieces that are supporting the floor.

I used three pieces of wood to fill in each side, although the dimensions of the 'bars' of the crate varied slightly according to availability. Start by filling in each end of the crate with pieces of timber. Use a wide piece of timber at the bottom to help retain straw, sawdust and chicken muck, but the subsequent two bars need not be quite so thick. I got away with using a 2¾ x 15¾" (7 x 40cm) piece at the bottom, with two 1½ x 15¾" (4 x 40cm) pieces spaced evenly above. Follow suit with the longitudinal rails, using wider ones at the bottom and narrower ones above. Again I was down to using scrap at this point and ended up with 38¼ x 3½, 38¼

Build It!....

x 2 and 38¼ x ¾" (or 97 x 9, 97 x 5 and 97 x 2cm) pieces for each side. You'll note that the long bars have to be a little less than a metre in length to fit inside of the ends. Fix the bars in place using nails, screws, glue or whatever else suits. Make sure that any nails that protrude through two pieces of wood and out the other side have their points flattened. A good way to do this is with two hammers; hold one hammer head firm against the head of the nail whilst using the other hammer to bash the protruding point on the other side of the plank(s).

The top of the poultry crate was cut out of an existing (block

footed) pallet so that all the planks and supports were already intact. To be honest, the top was cut at the start of the project which had some degree of influence over the sizing of the rest of the design. Before the top was screwed in place between the uprights, a little work was carried out to make a simple door. The door was simply one plank removed from the top and cut to 12" (30cm) in length. By situating the cuts for the door so that one of them was over another plank (see photo), this provided a backstop for the door to prevent it from opening inwards. The

crate top was installed before finishing work was carried out on the simple door. A hinge was screwed onto one end of the 12" (30cm) door and onto the crate top. In the closed position the 'door' rests on an underlying plank. A wooden turn-buckle was added to keep the door plank shut. Because there is a little sideways movement on a single plank anchored to a single hinge, some small wooden blocks were added as guides to either side of the opening end of the door. This addition ensures that rampant captive chickens cannot force the single bar door sideways and effect an escape.

As stated at the beginning, the crate got an airing within days of finishing it. The birds it held captive were not overly large, but if one wanted to carry smaller birds then extra bars could easily be added to the cage. Although the birds could easily get their heads out of the top of the crate, the spacing of timber was such that the gaps were not wide enough for them to push their 'shoulders' (or whatever you call the bit where the wings meet the body) through.

19. Bucket

I had this urge (that maybe ended up as a scourge) to make a wooden bucket. What I ended up with I think you'll agree looks very nice but it isn't exactly a bucket – it definitely doesn't hold water. Perhaps you could use it as another flaming planting tub? I had toyed with the idea of using it to salt pork but as I hadn't got it

Build It!....

① MARK AND CUT A CIRCLE ×2

② GLUE ONE CIRCLE TOGETHER

③ MARK AND CUT HOOP SECTIONS

④ ADD PLANKS TO THE BASE

⑤ GLUE HOOP IN PLACE

⑥ ADD THE CLOSING PLANKS

photographed properly at the time I didn't bother in case I ruined it. I think that overall it will make a splendid and unusual waste paper basket for my office. It does look useful but if you make one you will have to cook up your own uses for it.

If you want to make a bucket you'll need some PU wood glue and some wood filler, maybe more of that than pallets. First, decide what sort of diameter bucket you want to make. To be honest, the decision was made for me by the proximity of a 10" (25.5cm) diameter circular plastic pot that I could draw round. Begin by making up two pieces of wood that will provide you with two wooden discs of 10" (25.5cm) or whatever your chosen diameter. To do this, lay three pieces of plank side by side, put your template on top and draw a circle around it. Mark your boards so that you know which edge glues to which and then cut along your markings with a jigsaw or fretsaw. You will be left with three segments of a circular piece of wood that can be glued together. Use PU glue along the seams and leave it to set on a flat surface with a weight on top of it so that the wooden disc dries flat.

The second disc should not be

68

glued together in the same manner as we are trying to make a wooden hoop to go inside the bucket. Start as per the first disc by butting up three planks and marking a circle over them. Draw a second circle inside the first one. The diameter of the second circle should be about 2" (5cm) less than the first one. By carefully cutting along both of these lines, you will end up with several pieces that, when glued together, will produce a hoop about 1" (25mm) thick and with a 10" (25mm) diameter. It goes without saying that care must be taken in the glueing process to ensure that your hoop ends up reasonably true. It will help if you mark all the corresponding joints before you actually cut the segments of hoop out of your three pieces of plank.

Measuring around the base plate of your container you will find that if it is 10" (25.5cm) in diameter, it will need about 31" (0.8m) worth of planks around its edge. I cut my planks to 13½" (34.5cm) in length for some obscure reason; I think that this figure probably just corresponded to the shortest length of a load of offcuts I had sitting around.

I have neglected to mention that I planed all the timber for this project so that I would end up with a tidy looking indoor container. I cut and planed twelve and a bit planks for the sides of the bucket out of 3" (75mm) wide pallet planks. You wouldn't want to use a wider plank as you'd end up with less of a bucket and more of a polyhedron. Prior to fixing any of the planks to the bucket I used a plane and shaved all the edges of the planks. This was not done with any degree of accuracy, but it did ensure that the planks all butted together more closely and gave a better overall finish.

All the planks were attached to the base with a single central nail and PU glue. After the first plank was in its correct place, glue was added to the next plank at the bottom and along one side. Planks were put in place, nailed and glued to the adjoining plank one at a time, working around the base. To make this easier all the planks had a nail driven into them prior to being glued and offered into position. As the planks were added, care was taken to ensure that they remained perpendicular (upright) to the base and that the integrity of the circle was maintained. When about two-thirds of the planks were in place the hoop was glued into position about 4" (10cm) down from the top. Glue was used around the entire diameter of the hoop and clamps were used to hold the hoop whilst the glue dried. The last thin closing plank was measured to fit the remaining gap and was then nailed and glued in place.

The project was finished off with some pine-coloured wood filler applied to the seams of the container with a dirty finger. When the filler had dried, the container was given a light sanding to remove excess PU glue and blend any protruding areas of wood or filler.

The finished container will probably be given an exterior coating of antique wax that I have kicking around in a cupboard somewhere. Although I never intended to end up with a bin, it's a jolly nice one and it was only made from small wooden offcuts.

20. Chest

I have one very large heavy chest that was made for us out of pallets by a friend. I envisaged making another smaller version that could be used as an occasional coffee table. My inspiration for the idea came from a very nice little antique chest in a neighbour's house.

Now that mine is finished, it looks OK but it is not antique and nor does it have dovetail corners. I think the reality is that I've maybe captured more of the Argos (budget catalogue business) feel rather than the antique farmhouse feel. You may chuckle.

The overall dimensions of my chest are 29½ x 13¾ x 11¾" (75 x 35 x 30cm). These figures are undeniably more to do with the availability of decent long planks than any precise maths. All the chest sides are three planks high and the floor is made from planks and is screwed on from underneath. The lid for the chest is made out of four planks and is held together by two lengths of wood screwed to the inner side. The lid is attached to the chest by two metal hinges.

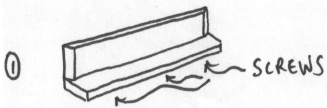

I made the sides and body of my chest with all of the plank ends mitre cut. This means that the plank ends are all cut at 45 degrees so that no end grain is visible on the outside corners of the chest.

Build It!....

If you are not able to cut all your planks in this manner it needn't stop you making the chest. Simply use butt joints at the corners and accept that the finished dimensions of the chest will be a little different. I planed all of the planks for this project so that it didn't end up looking like something from the back of a scrapyard.

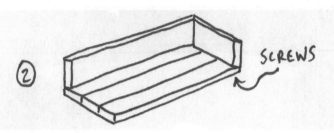

Cut six pieces of 4" (10cm) wide plank to 29½" (75cm) in length and six more to 13¾" (35cm). It's up to you whether you mitre cut the plank ends or not. To do this you will need either a mitre saw or a mitre box saw guide (they're only a couple of quid). The next step is to prepare the timber for the base. The base measures 29½ x 13¾" (75 x 35cm) so you will need enough planks lying side by side to achieve that dimension. If you are using normal butted up joints on your chest, either the ends will have to be reduced slightly to fit onto the base or the base will have to be increased slightly in width to accommodate the extra wood in the joints. Inevitably, with either construction style, you're going to have to cut one smaller base plank to fit anyway.

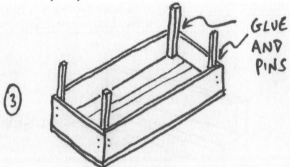

I used a combination of PU glue and 1½" (40mm) wood screws to fix the baseboards to the side planks. Join one of the long sides to a long baseboard. The sides are all situated on top of the base planks. All the screws are from the bottom up through the floor and into the sides. After sticking a side and a floor piece together, add the short ends and screw them to the first baseboard plank. Don't be unduly worried about gluing too early. I only added glue in the corner joints when I was happy that the whole thing was forming up squarely.

MAKE LID AS PER THE PHOTO

When the floor was finished and screwed to the side planks I added some glue into the joints. You will need four lengths of timber 1" square (20–25mm²) and 11" (28cm) long to help reinforce the corners of the chest. Using these lengths of timber, some panel pins, a couple of clamps and lots of PU glue, I built up the chest using an 11" (28cm) piece in each corner. By working around the four sides with my glue and panel pins and clamps to hold things in place, it only took about twenty minutes to get the rest of the chest in place.

The lid of the chest is made so that it has a slight lip (up to ½" or 10mm) on the long front (nicest looking) side and the two short ends. Again, you will probably need three planks plus one that you've cut down in width. Measure your chest to make sure you're cutting the lid planks to the correct size and include an extra ¾" (2cm) if you want the described cosmetic lip. The planks are fastened together with two 11¾" (30cm) long pieces of wood screwed across them.

Build It!....

The bracing pieces I used were just plank offcuts cut to size and reduced to about 1¼" (3cm) in width. I fastened my bracing pieces to the underside of the lid using screws and glue. Position them about ¾" (20mm) inward of the ends. Position the bracing bars so that they don't interfere with the closed position of the chest lid.

The last items to be added were a pair of hinges. I used a sharp pocketknife to cut a small recess for each hinge in the upper edge of the chest side. I attached the hinges into these recesses and used small ½– ¾" (15–20mm) screws to secure them. Aligning the chest lid and fixing it to the hinges will always be easier said than done.

There were a few holes in the chest that required some filler but I've left some of the original nail holes as they add what little air of rusticity the chest has. If you are using filler, get some with a bit of stain in it as plain white just looks a mess. I have given it a bit of a sanding down but as yet have not painted or treated it. Light softwoods do age over time but can end up just looking dirty if not treated. The best method of treatment is to paint pale softwood with a light antique-type wood stain and then apply some wax afterwards. You can get this type of treatment from most DIY stores. I bought a large tin of antique wax ages ago and it's done a lot of jobs, looks good and there's still plenty left in the tin.

21. Sawhorse

I'd always wanted a sawhorse, and having never found the time to make one I thought the idea was worthy of inclusion in this compendium, so I got sketching. For those who chop or burn wood, a sawhorse will hold long logs, branches or timbers whilst you cut them into sections with your chainsaw. Not a difficult project to construct by any means, it has only ten pieces of timber, two bolts and twenty-six screws in it. I was working with a pallet that had some planks of 5½" (14cm) in width and almost 1" (25mm) in thickness. Anything over 4" (10cm) in width with close to ¾" (20mm) in thickness would do. I used four lengths of 4' (1.2m approx.) for the crosses on either end of the sawhorse and I used four lengths of 3' (91cm) timber for the horizontal crosspieces. Two short battens of about 2' (60cm) in length were used to lock the two halves together.

FORM TWO CROSSES

JOIN THE TWO X's TOGETHER

ADD THE REMAINDER OF THE REQUIRED PLANKS

ONE LAST PIECE ACROSS THE BOTTOM PLANKS LOCKS THE 'HORSE' IN POSITION

Start by constructing the two crosses. First make sure that your four pieces of timber are all trimmed to the same length. Take two of the pieces of

TAKE CARE WHEN USING POWER SAWS

Build It!....

timber and lay them one on top of the other so that the ends are level. Mark a point 29–30" (75cm approx.) from one end of the planks and drill a hole on the centre line through both of them. I drilled a ¼" (6mm) hole because I have a large supply of ¼" (6mm) bolts. The two planks are then bolted together through this hole, making a cross that you can then open out into an X shape. Having made two crosses, one for each end, it's now a task of joining the two ends together with some horizontal pieces of timber.

I laid both crosses down (closed) balanced on their respective edges. A 3' (91cm) plank was screwed between the two of them. This first plank was attached to the crosses about 4" (10cm) from what will be ground level when the sawhorse is upright. Make sure this first plank is screwed on at 90 degrees to the uprights. Refer to the diagrams if confused. Each horizontal plank needs to be screwed to the outward facing plank of one end and the inward side of the other end. Use two or three decent wood screws at each joint. Anything between 1½ and 1¾" (40 and 45mm) in length will be ideal. Carefully turn over the whole affair and add a plank to the other side. Try to make sure you're assembling the device as squarely as possible. Working on a flat surface helps a lot in achieving this. Also, ensure that you are screwing the horizontal planks to the correct legs. If you get it wrong then the sawhorse will not open when you stand it up.

With the two crosses made and now joined together by a couple of planks, you should be able to carefully open up the sawhorse so that it stands on its own. A further two planks can now be added. Screw these on, one on either side, just below the crosses. Lastly, some pieces of approximately 2' (60cm) are required to lock the two sides into a fixed position. I screwed these two pieces of wood across the gap between the lower horizontal planks.

The sawhorse was a classic example of something that, in theory, took less than an hour to make. What did take time was trying to extract four long planks with lots of nails in them. In total it took me about two and a half hours to salvage enough of my chosen pallet to make this item; hardly what you'd call economy of effort. Happy sawing

Other Ideas

This short book is a mere scratch on the surface when it comes to the thousands of things you could do with pallet wood if you have the time and feel so inclined. Here are some extra ideas that you can take, adapt and turn into more pallet projects.

Garden Trays

About halfway through two of the described projects I did consider just making some simple trays and carriers that could be used for garden work. I seem to recall seeing some nice large wooden trays at one of my uncle's chateau that were employed for drying onions on. Cut a few lengths of plank to 2' (61cm) in length. Lay the lengths side by side and nail on two cross members across their collective width. Turn the lot over and you have a floor. Another two 2' (61cm) lengths will give you some sides for your tray. The remaining two shorter sides will have to be measured to fit as we are now only hypothesising. You can turn a tray into a general tidy and carrier by simply adding a length of batten down the centre line. PS. My uncle doesn't really have a chateau but he does have the nice wooden trays and he does dry onions on them.

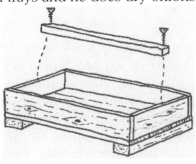

Build It!....

Bird Nest Box

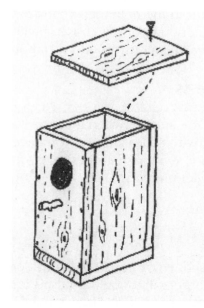

Whilst I wouldn't claim to be the most avid of birdwatchers, I do recognise that a world without birds would be a very dull place indeed. The sad truth is that, like many other species, we have encroached on their natural habitats and kicked them out of their homes. Whilst your house might be very comfortable, for many species of bird your property is less suited for nesting than the original barren site. Make a nest box and you might entice a family of birds back onto your homestead. I did have some 5½" (14cm) wide planks. Four 7" (18cm) lengths of this plank would easily make four sides which would all nail together. Fix on a floor to one of the open ends made out of whatever you have available. Cut a 1½" (40mm) hole about 2" (5cm) down from the top edge for the birds to get in and out. Drill a small ½" (12mm) hole beneath this and insert a piece of stick as a perch. The last thing it needs is a roof. Make this with an overlap to keep the rain off. Nail the box up somewhere suitable with a substantial nail. The roof can be fixed to the body with a single screw when the box is in position.

Go-kart!

I did have it in my mind to produce some plans for a soapbox-style go-kart, but I wasn't able to get my hands on a decent set of wheels in time, but I reckon I could produce a cracking racer out of two half decent pallets. Use an existing section of pallet to make the seat area (cut down into sections as described for the rustic chair). Use the harder wood that's often used as the spacer between the pallet planks to make the front steering axle, the rear axle and the structure that joins the body to the front axle. Discard anything with cracks in it and use nuts, bolts and washers for strong joints. You can buy ⅜ and ½" (10 and 12mm) threaded rod from plenty of hardware shops, or cut down some long coach bolts to make stub axles which can be bolted to the underside of the wooden axles. I can't comment on wheels, "When I were a lad there wus allus an urld pram ter be 'ad". Sadly babies' prams with wheels suitable for making racers are now few and far between. I recently spied a set of four pneumatic wheels on eBay that only made about fifteen pounds – that's probably the answer.

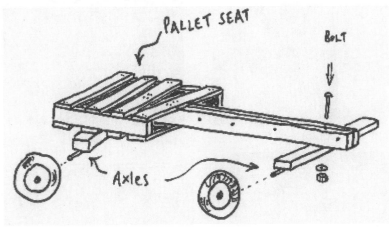

Toys

Although I have some young kids of my own, wooden toys were not something I had initially considered. Ron has a colossal collection of wooden toys fashioned for his grandchildren. All the toys are made out of pallet wood with a few other pieces of scrap thrown in for good measure. Have a look at some of the photos to get some ideas of your own. Probably the easiest project to make is a wooden aeroplane as it only requires outlines marked and cut out of pieces of pallet plank. The most impressive of the creations is the wooden timber truck where even the trailer wheels are individually made out of pieces of timber. Whilst making toys is a specialist area of woodworking, you have to admit that it's quite impressive that these items were made from discarded wooden pallets

Build It!....

Photos courtesy of RH

Sheds

If it's possible to make a model of the Taj Mahal out of matchsticks, then it's equally possible to build something big out of pallets. The best example I could cite of this was a video I once saw on the internet of a group of lads who built a full size 'Wall of Death' on a farm. The whole thing was made from pallets and lined with sheet ply and they even got to riding mopeds around it.

During the writing of this book I did get a phone call to say that Ron had built a chicken house out of pallets. When I got to his house I was gobsmacked to see a walk-in 8 x 10' (2.44 x 3.05m) chicken

Photo courtesy of RH

shed standing in his front yard. The most amusing bit is that he lives in a cul-de-sac: the neighbours were probably expecting a new free-range enterprise. What Ron had actually done was get his hands on a particular type of pallet used for carrying roofing sheets. These pallets are in fact 8' (2.44m) long and so contain a fair quantity of reasonable quality timber which is more than suitable for building a large shed. Whilst we are not going into any detail on this project, the pictures will illustrate what can be done if you have enough time and can get your hands on enough pallets.

Picture Frame

USE GLUE ON JOINTS

FAT PIG

Another daft idea that was in the running but didn't make the final cut came from an inspiration I once got from reading a book on making furniture from recyclables. A rustic picture frame is relatively easy to make, providing that you can measure, mark and cut 45 degree angles accurately. I'd suggest you'd want at least partially planed wood. PU glue is ideal for sticking picture frames together, but just remember to do it on a level surface.

Build It!....

Hanging Shelves

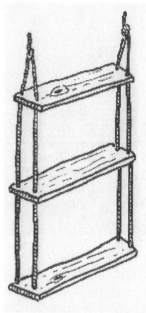

It's amazing the junk that runs through my head late at night. It's now not far off midnight and I've just re-invented the wheel again. If you've got some nice wide planks 5" (12cm) or wider, you could easily fashion a set of hanging shelves. All you need is some pieces of plank, perhaps three lengths of 2' (60cm) and some decent ⅜–½" (8–12mm) rope. Stack all your three shelves in a pile and drill a hole (the same diameter as your rope) a little inside each corner. You now have three shelves, all with a hole in each corner. It's now a case of careful threading and rope work. You'll need four lengths of rope and the ability to tie simple overhand knots. Tie a stopper knot in each rope and thread on the first plank. Leave a 1' (30cm) gap, tie another knot, thread on the next plank..... You get the idea? It does take a bit of adjusting of all the knots to get the planks level, but it makes an effective shelf set. Tie the ropes in two pairs at the top so that the shelf is hung from two points.

Bike Rack

This was Ron's idea, not mine, but he did make a very nice example which might benefit anyone wishing to keep their bicycles tidy in the garage. Decide how many bikes you want to park. In this instance we'll say three. This design holds the front wheels of each bike so that the machine is kept standing in an upright position. Measure the width of each bike, pedal tip to pedal tip, and the tyre width. For the sake of argument, allow 20" (50cm approx.) per bike and a 3" (8cm approx.) gap which should suffice for most bike tyres. Make a base 40" (1.0m) long by about 16" (40cm) wide. Use lengths of plank mounted on three short cross pieces. The length isn't critical, but it might be possible to cut an existing pallet down to this dimension. Make up two similar base-type sections. Firmly fix one section as an upright along the back of the other section. Use three pairs of planks to make bars to hold the bike wheels. The pairs of planks used to hold the wheels will need to be between 16 and 20" (40 and 50cm) long and would be best at about 3"

BiKE RACK

(75mm) wide. You'll have to measure the exact diagonal gap when you have finished the sides and back. All the ends of these six bars will have to be cut at 45 degrees so that they will fit into the rack. Position the bars so that they are 3" (75mm) apart. A pair of bars can then be fixed at each end of the rack and a pair in the middle.

Subsequent to this design I have wondered whether you could simply use a section of cut down pallet and adjust the spacing of some of the planks to trap bike wheels in between the gaps. That would be very quick and simple indeed.

Rabbit Hutch

Whilst I'm going to offer little more than the idea, it's not a million miles away from the poultry crate project with three sides and a top that have been fully boarded. One side needs bars so that 'Bugs' can see out. Make a run as per the raised bed idea.

Hay Rack

When I warble on about lengths of batten, I only mean planking that's been thinned down to about 2" (50mm) wide. You could write a book on building stuff from battening alone. For anyone that eats hay, a hay rack is a nicety that can easily be knocked together out of half a dozen planks. Make up two solid sides out of pallet planks. Make your rack about 29½" (75cm) deep and the

Build It!....

same wide. The opening at the top of the rack should be at least 1' (30cm) deep. Refer to the sketch diagram to see how it fits together. This unit would be best tied to a suitable gate or beam.

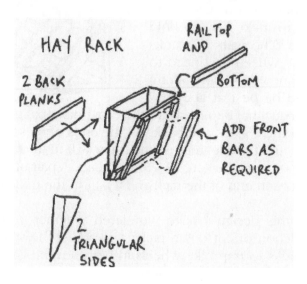

Lamb Creep Feeder

This is a project that I fully intend to make in the near future as my flock of sheep is just about to start lambing. A creep feeder is useful for feeding concentrates to lambs. It is constructed so that the adult sheep are too wide to enter into the feeding area. The advantage of offering lambs creep feed is that it keeps growth rates going very early and late on in the season when the grass is at a lower nutritional content. The creep would be made from four pallets, one of which should have its planking altered so that there are no gaps larger than that required for your breed of lambs. There needs to be a wooden trough attached to the rear side of the creep and there needs to be a ceiling over this trough so that the food doesn't get rained on and turned into mush. As I said, I haven't got around to making one just yet, but the finished item will closely resemble the rough design as illustrated.

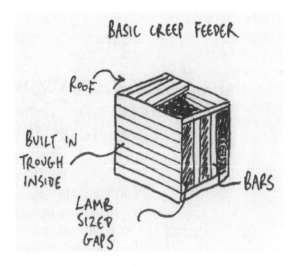

Boot Remover

Have a look at the photo and you will soon appreciate that some of the simplest ideas are the best. Two pieces of scrap are all it took to make a boot remover, a very useful item for taking off one's muddy boots without getting dirty hands. You'll need a piece of plank 4–5" (10–12cm) in width. Take one 12" (30cm) length of plank, cut a U out of the end of it and add a short length of wood underneath to act as a pivot. The only noteworthy point is getting the U shape to be the correct size for the encapsulated heel of your foot.

Photo courtesy of RH

Steps and Ladders

If you have a pallet that is made from very thick timber you have the basic ingredients to make a simple set of steps or ladders useful for cleaning windows or reaching high items in the garage or workshop. A set of steps comprises of the two long risers, the steps themselves

Build It!....

and the wooden blocks for the steps to rest on. If you just try screwing steps between the uprights the likelihood is that when you stand on a step it will break. Mount each step on small wooden blocks that are firmly screwed to the inside of the risers.

STEPS

BLOCK SUPPORTS SCREWED TO THE RISERS

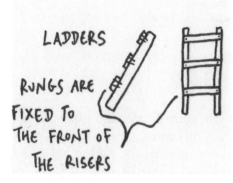

LADDERS

RUNGS ARE FIXED TO THE FRONT OF THE RISERS

You can also make a simple short ladder, providing it's not too wide. Make the risers from the strong wooden spacing bars, and the rungs about 14" (35cm) long from the thickest pieces of flaw-free plank that you have. Thin these pieces of plank down to about 2" (50mm) wide. Nail, screw or bolt these rungs to the front of your side timbers (not in between). Use two decent screws per joint or alternatively ¼" (6mm) coach bolts.

Sea Chest/Blanket Box

I thought the first bloke I ever came across who made things out of pallets was a bit crackers. Why, I wondered, would anybody bother when you could get eight foot by four foot sheets of plywood for about fifteen quid. I still think that wood is not valued highly enough and is unreasonably cheap. Little did I know that several years later I'd be writing some sort of an epistle on knocking up stuff out of what I was then deriding. Aside from chicken houses, fencing and the usual run-of-the-mill stuff that can be made from pallet wood, Pat Crawford was the first person to demonstrate to me that you could turn fairly rough timber into attractive and usable day-to-day

86

furniture. Pat made a series of nice, well made wooden chests out of pallet wood and bequeathed one to us as a present. Although I've used the text before, it's worthy of inclusion here as well.

The pallet used in this instance consisted of wooden staves approximately ¾" (17mm) thick and 7½" (190mm) in width.

The base measures 35½ x 16½" (90 x 42cm). Planks cut to 35½" (90cm) in length are simply nailed to three pieces of 16½" (42cm) long timber. The sides of the box are made individually before being assembled. The small sides measure 19¼" (49cm) long x 18½" (47cm) deep. The long sides are 35½ x 18½" (90 x 47cm) and the top is 35½ x 14⅛" (90 x 36cm). The sides are fixed to the base and each other with suitable screws and nails. The sides are fastened to the edges of the base and do not sit on top of it. Strap hinges are

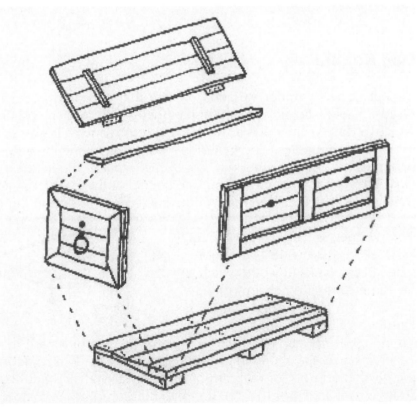

Build It!....

used to secure the lid to an additional plank fixed to the top of the box. The top edges of the box are finished with a patterned 15¾ x ⬜" (400 x10mm) architrave. By protruding the architrave above the top edge of the box, a recess is formed into which the lid closes. An architrave is also used to cover the joints on all four corners.

The box was finished with a dark wood stain, steel ring handles were fitted at each end for carrying, chains were fitted inside to limit the opening of the lid and Pat also made a lovely wooden clasp and pin for the front, which is probably a little beyond the purposes of this book.

A 1" (2.5cm) diameter hole was drilled in each end and two at a regular intervals in the front which add to the overall effect, but also contribute to the airing of the intended purpose: a box for storing linen and blankets.

Dog Kennel

This project is a minor variation on one that appeared in the first Build It! book. In the romantic times before there were children, we got a dog. Well, it was a sheepdog actually, and as it was a little puppy with boundless energy I didn't want it permanently indoors, so I built it a smart kennel out of sawmill offcuts. The kennel cost very little, but it was only during the course of these pallet-making tribulations that I realised that I could have made it for nothing.

The kennel is 39⅜" (1.0m) long by 23⅝" (0.6m) wide. The floor is made from planks of wood which sit on three 23⅝" (0.6m) long blocks. It would be easy to use part of an existing pallet for the floor and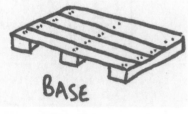

BASE

simply fill in the gaps between the planks as demonstrated in the bench project. The wooden blocks help to keep the kennel floor off the ground and out of the damp. The sides are 23⅝" (0.6m) high and the roof apex is 33½" (0.85m) high measured from the floor.

Make up the side panels using planks. Use a 19¾" (0.5m) length of batten across the boards at the ends of each panel to hold the plank sides together. This timber should be positioned so that when the side is nailed into place, the bottom end of the batten sits on the kennel floor. The side panels protrude downward below the kennel floor level to ground level.

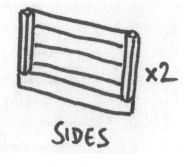

SIDES

BRACING STRIPS

The completed side panels can be nailed onto the woodwork that is supporting the kennel floor. Join the two sides together by nailing one 23☐" (0.6m) strip across the top edge at each end.

This will help to brace the two sides and give supports to attach further timber to. Above these crosspieces you need to form a triangle of wood that will support the roof and the ends. Cut two lengths of narrow plank to 15¾" (40cm) and mitre the ends so that the pieces will fit together to form a triangle above the cross member that's bracing the kennel sides.

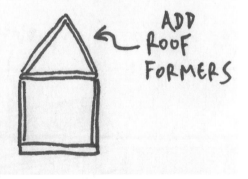

ADD ROOF FORMERS

The entrance is formed using planks in a vertical rather than a horizontal plane. Use a plank between 4 and 6" (10 and 15cm) wide at each side of the doorway to close the front end down a little. Fill in the top triangle above the doorway with vertical boarding and do the same for the rear end. If you wish to have a smaller door, bring

Build It!....

the cladding down a little lower. Use a horizontal piece of plank at the bottom edge of the doorway.

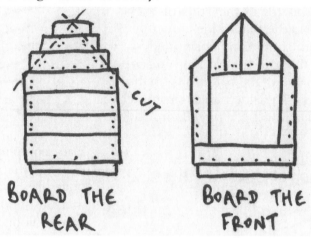

BOARD THE
REAR

BOARD THE
FRONT

The roof can be made up of scrap wood but may need an internal length of timber to bring the ridge together. Finish the roofing job with a covering of felt that slightly overlaps the kennel sides. Treat the kennel with a proprietary wood treatment product.

RIDGE BAR

BOARD THE ROOF

The End

And there, ladies and gents, we shall leave it. It's been an experience, but the trouble with writing books on making stuff from pallets is the amount of time needed to take them to pieces. Whilst it is a worthwhile timber source for much needed personal projects, it is also time consuming when one has the PC in one hand and a list of experimental ideas in the other. There will be yet another Build It! project shortly. Certainly this will be a more general volume akin to the first one. I have even generated some nice plans for a large canoe that I hope to build and sail soon – I'm only pleased to say it won't be made from pallets.

Build It!....

Further Reading

I have an eclectic collection of books on farming, smallholding and DIY. Here are some titles I have found helpful that may be of interest to readers of this book. If you have enjoyed this title, you might like to know that this is volume two in what could prove to be an extensive series. Happy reading.

Cobleigh R. Handy Farm Devices and How to Make Them . Available on Amazon. Note: The original sentiment is good but as it was first printed in 1909, the ideas are very dated.

Jackson, Day. Complete DIY Manual. Collins. (An excellent basic DIY book).

Jacobs J. Build It!. DIY Projects for Farmers, Smallholders and Gardeners. The Good Life Press .

Seymour J. The Complete Book of Self Sufficiency. DK. (The smallholding classic).

UK Suppliers

Howarth Timber – My local timber supplier and pallet sponsor. They have branches around the UK.

Screwfix (www.screwfix.co.uk) Part of the Kingfisher group (also includes B&Q). Mail order, internet and trade-counter based firm; very cheap on hardware, plumbing and ironmongery.

Ebay (www.ebay.co.uk) – needs no introduction, there's still bargains to be had.

Build It!

DIY Projects for Farmers, Smallholders and Gardeners

ISBN: 978 9 90487 132 3
PRICE: £12.99
AUTHOR: Joe Jacobs

Using recycled materials wherever possible, engineer and smallholder Joe Jacobs provides clear, step-by-step instructions for over 50 DIY projects for both inside and outside the home farm. Joe guides you through the equipment, the tools, the materials and the plans, all complete with measurements and instructions.

The projects include a polytunnel, beehives, chicken arks and runs, gates, hurdles and fencing, cloches, feedbins, incubators, nesting boxes and renewable energy projects including solar panels and plenty more, making this an essential book for any keen enthusiast with a basic knowledge of construction.

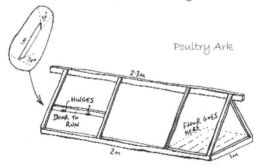

Poultry Ark

Build It! by Joe Jacobs is published by The Good Life Press,
PO Box 536, Preston, PR2 9ZY

www.goodlifepress.co.uk

93

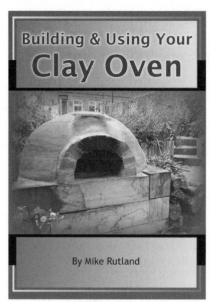

By Mike Rutland

Buildng and Using Your Clay Oven

By Mike Rutland

Mike Rutland shows you how to make the ultimate architectural garden accessory – a clay oven.

Home made bread, freshly baked and still warm to serve at the BBQ; pizzas served at the kids' parties or even a slow roasted joint of lamb. All are possible with Mike's step-by-step instructions on building and using your own clay oven.

The contents include the history of the clay oven, why make and use a clay oven, the choice of materials, preparing the site for work, making the base, making and maintaining the oven and recipes including breads, pizzas and roasted meats as well as a section covering dismantling and recycling the oven at the end of its life.

And as for that slow roasted lamb – well here's the perfect recipe for you: take your joint, rub in some olive oil, stud the meat with a knife point, fill the voids made with the knife point with a piece of anchovy wrapped in a piece of rosemary and simply place it into the middle of the oven, shutting the door behind. Then simply leave it for around 3-4 hours.

The initial cooking will take place in the first half hour as the lamb "sizzles" in the heat, then, as the oven cools, the lamb will slow cook gently, the oil lubricating and the anchovies melting away into nothing more than a salty highlight. Take out the lamb, slice it thickly and serve with a good wedge of bread (cooked in the oven before the lamb, of course!) or leave it to cool and enjoy the cold cuts the next day. The lamb will not need much in the way of carving as it simply falls off the bone, making the shoulder the ideal clay oven roast as not only is it usually a pain to carve with the blade bone in the way, but it is also a hard working muscle with a good marbling of fat which will cook through and baste the meat in its own juices as it cooks slowly, helping to break down the muscle fibres to make a tender and succulent Sunday roast for those summer afternoons eating alfresco.

ISBN 978 1 90487 1 972

 The Good Life Press
The Old Pigsties, Clifton Fields
Lytham Road
Preston PR4 0xg
01772 652693

The Good Life Press Ltd. is a family run business specialising in publishing a wide range of titles for the smallholder, 'goodlifer' and farmer. We also publish **Home Farmer,** the monthly magazine for anyone who wants to grab a slice of the good life - whether they live in the country or the city.

Other Titles of interest:

A Guide to Traditional Pig Keeping by Carol Harris
An Introduction to Keeping Cattle by Peter King
An Introduction to Keeping Sheep by J. Upton/D. Soden
Build It! by Joe Jacobs
Craft Cider Making by Andrew Lea
Flowerpot Farming by Jayne Neville
How to Butcher Livestock and Game by Paul Peacock
Making Country Wines, Ales and Cordials by Brian Cook
Making Jams and Preserves by Diana Sutton
Precycle! by Paul Peacock
Raising Chickens for Eggs and Meat by Mike Woolnough
Showing Sheep by Sue Kendrick
Talking Sheepdogs by Derek Scrimgeour
The Bread and Butter Book by Diana Sutton
The Cheese Making Book by Paul Peacock
The Frugal Life by Piper Terrett
The Medicine Garden by Rachel Corby
The Pocket Guide to Wild Food by Paul Peacock
The Polytunnel Companion by Jayne Neville
The Sausage Book by Paul Peacock
The Secret Life of Cows by Rosamund Young
The Smoking and Curing Book by Paul Peacock
The Urban Farmer's Handbook by Paul Peacock

www.goodlifepress.co.uk
www.homefarmer.co.uk